THE
DOCUMENTARY
MOVIEMAKING
COURSE

The starter guide to documentary filmmaking

Kevin J. Lindenmuth

A QUARTO BOOK

First edition for North America
published in 2010 by
Barron's Educational Series, Inc.

Copyright © 2010 Quarto Inc.

All inquiries should be addressed to:
Barron's Educational Series, Inc.
250 Wireless Boulevard
Hauppauge, New York 11788
www.barronseduc.com

Library of Congress Control No.:
2010928082
ISBN 13: 978-0-7641-4503-2
ISBN 10: 0-7641-4503-7

QUAR.DMC

Conceived, designed, and produced by
Quarto Publishing plc
The Old Brewery
6 Blundell Street
London N7 9BH

Project Editor: Emma Poulter
Designer: Tanya Devonshire Jones
Design Assistant: Saffron Stocker
Illustrator: Kuo Kang Chen
Picture Researcher: Sarah Bell
Copyeditor: Claire Waite Brown
Proofreader: Liz Dalby
Art Director: Caroline Guest

Creative Director: Moira Clinch
Publisher: Paul Carslake

Color separation in Hong Kong by
Modern Age Repro House Ltd
Printed in China by 1010 printing
International Ltd

9 8 7 6 5 4 3 2 1

Contents

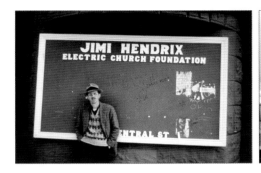

No subject too small
Documentaries embrace a huge range of subject areas from art to science to music (left to right): Crumb *(1995),* A Brief History of Time *(1992), and* Proceed and Be Bold *(2008).*

Introduction

A documentary is a means of observing life and interpreting the world, and of all the forms of video and film production, it lends itself to the widest variety of subjects and styles. Since its ultimate purpose is to "document reality," it could be about anything that is nonfiction.

The term "documentary" was first coined in the mid-1920s, primarily to refer to instructional films and travelogs, which had previously been referred to as "actuality" films. Perhaps the most well-known early documentary is Robert J. Flaherty's *Nanook of the North* (1922), which depicts the primitive life of an Inuit. More recent popular documentaries include Al Gore's *An Inconvenient Truth* and the nature documentary *March of the Penguins*.

In the twenty-first century, documentaries have become much more complex and popular than those early travelogs from nearly a century ago. Practically every DVD of a movie has a "making of" documentary included and, thanks to the advent of digital video technology, it is now possible to create an entire feature-length documentary with minimal crew and resources.

I began my career producing and directing narrative features, and though some of the creative process is different, much of it remains the same. Surprisingly, I discovered that my style of putting together fictional films translated well to creating programs about real life, proving that the attitude of the director is integral to the uniqueness of the documentary. Documentaries are meant to both educate and entertain. How you choose to do this depends on what you personally bring to the production as its creator.

In this book, I use my hands-on experience of producing, shooting, and editing television programs, to guide you through the process of creating a successful documentary, from start to finish. Enjoy!

Kevin J. Lindenmuth

About this book

This book is an essential, no-nonsense guide to becoming a documentary producer, from generating an interesting topic, to organizing the production, and ultimately presenting your finished program to a television or DVD distributor and the worldwide market.

The first section of the book will help you to come up with ideas for subjects and make sure you avoid certain pitfalls. Then you will learn about the equipment and technical requirements necessary to put your vision to video, how to adequately cover your subject, and the best way in which to interview people. Will your production be able to attract investors or obtain sponsors? Or is it something you are willing to self-fund in order for it to see the light of day? All of these various funding options are discussed to help you make the best decision, which of course hinges on what your ultimate goal is for your documentary.

The remaining sections will help you plan your workload and organize shoots and interviews, advise you on how best to put it all together, and suggest channels for publicizing and ways to achieve the ultimate goal of getting the film shown. The series of assignments throughout will allow you to determine what type of documentary is "right" for you and help you to establish your own individualistic style.

SECTION 2
EQUIPMENT AND TAPE FORMAT

Making a documentary half a century ago meant shooting on film, an extremely costly process that involved renting the camera equipment, purchasing the film stock, and paying for the processing. Back then equipment was also cumbersome, requiring several people to operate everything, from pulling focus to monitoring the audio. The most nerve-wracking part was that you were not sure how your footage would turn out until you got it back from the film processing lab, which could be weeks or months later. Video was cheaper than film, but it would be decades before it was a readily acceptable format for professional independent productions.

The 42 lessons are organized into six sections

Previews the lessons in the section

Technique files demonstrate moviemaking methods

Packed with tips and insider tricks

The objective of each lesson is identified

Lesson assignments set the reader practical challenges

Lesson 20
How to get the most production value

The case studies follow the author as he plans, makes, then edits a documentary

Case study: *Shooting a documentary*

This first-person account gives the inside skinny on the logistics of making a documentary

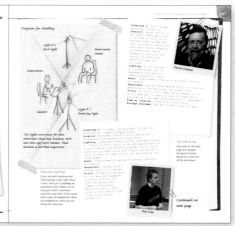

FINDING A SUBJECT AND STYLE

Documentaries are about people, places, and things that are real. In fact, they can be about virtually anything. Before you embark upon your production, you must determine what your film is to be about and how best to show your topic to your eventual audience. There is no right way to come up with a subject or particular style in which to convey it. There is also nothing wrong with emulating the types of documentaries you enjoy, as long as you bring your own energy and perspective to the film. What is important is to keep your eyes and ears open to all possibilities.

Subject

A subject can be social, cultural, historical, based on science/nature, or even a profile of an individual. A documentary can also have more than one topic. A subject you are passionate about, such as growing an organic garden in the inner city or skydiving in the desert, may make a good topic for a documentary. The organic garden may delve into the economics of the city and the politics involved in getting a permit to plant vegetables. The skydiving documentary might convey a religious element to the diver's experience. If your documentary is about new treatments for cancer it may be scientific in nature, but you can also debate the economic problems of sufferers who do not have health insurance. If you are having difficulty coming up with a topic that is to your liking, you may want to visit your local library to see what other documentaries are out there. Expose yourself to as many different types of documentaries as possible in preparation. This could give you the ideas and inspiration you need to get started.

Style

When carrying out research, you will immediately notice that different documentaries are put together in different ways, with varying styles used to communicate information. One program may have numerous sit-down interviews with experts on the particular subject, while another may consist of voice-over narration telling the viewer what is going on. The camera shots may be handheld, done from a tripod, or moving smoothly with the help of a Steadicam. One documentary may feature a great deal of computer graphic effects, while another may have minimal, bare-bones graphics. One may include edits every 20 seconds, while another may stay on single shots for minutes at a time. Simply choosing the type of documentary and the subject will in part determine your style.

CONTENTS

Lesson 1 : Types of documentaries

There are four types of documentaries: expository, observational, participatory, and the dramatic documentary. A single documentary may take the form of more than one of these broad types; this primarily depends on how interactive the documentary maker's approach is.

> > > **Assignment 1**

Write down five popular expository documentaries that immediately come to mind. What made these films memorable to you?

Sicko (2007)
The absurdity of some of the situations in Michael Moore's expository movie—such as the guy who had to choose which fingers he wanted re-attached because his health care wouldn't cover all the digits—in light of their seriousness, makes this documentary about the lack of health care in the U.S. extremely memorable.

Expository type

Expository documentaries tend to rely on verbal commentary. They try to persuade the viewer into taking a certain viewpoint, usually with a voice-over narration that addresses them directly. They also have an "omniscient point of view," which explains and defines the topic. This type of documentary is written, with the images and interviews serving to follow the text of the script. Examples are the *Meerkat Manor* series on Animal Planet, Morgan Spurlock's *30 Days*, A&E Network's *Biography*, and even *America's Most Wanted*.

This type of documentary often presents an argument to prove a point, such as "why aren't people conserving energy?," then suggests solutions. The problem/situation they present supplies the tension. The "hook" of the documentary is the need for a solution to the problem. Prime examples of this are *Flow*, about the global freshwater shortage, and *An Inconvenient Truth*, about global warming. Even Frank Capra's *Why We Fight* series, made during World War II, is expository, as is hinted in the title.

Expository documentaries have a linear flow to them, with a beginning, middle, and end. All of the images are chosen to illustrate and support the commentary, even if out of context. Likewise, with the people being interviewed, what they say supports the argument of the documentary. Even if there is no voice-over narration and the filmmaker is simply asking the interviewee questions, which they answer on-screen, this is still considered expository, because they are answering questions relevant to the gist of the documentary.

Expository documentaries have the strongest point of view and often deal with subjects relating to politics, activism, or some type of intervention. They want to persuade the viewer to agree with them.

Observational type

Observational documentaries can best be thought of as the opposite of the expository documentary. They are made with a minimum of intervention by the filmmaker, who basically remains as a "fly on the wall," seemingly invisible throughout the production. The documentary maker is simply there to observe life and let the viewer draw their own conclusions when they watch what is shown. If you are making an observational documentary about a day in the life of a group of bird-watchers seeking to spy a particularly rare bird, you would shoot them from the sidelines without any personal interaction with any of the members. You and the camera are strictly an observer. Then, although you may condense time in editing, you would still keep everything in the order in which it was shot.

With this type of documentary, the filmmaker takes far less of an active role in manipulating the content. There are no reenactments, no restaging, and no direct interviews. If people are heard talking, it is as if the viewer is overhearing their conversation as an observer. An observational documentary tries to unobtrusively document what is happening on-screen. You could say it's the most truthful and voyeuristic form of documentary making.

Many ethnographic films, which show a visual anthropology of human groups such as an isolated village of people in the Appalachians, tend to be this type of documentary. For that matter, anyone who has videotaped a wedding and stayed in the background has made an observational documentary. Even concert films, if they are shot live, could be considered observational documentaries.

March of the Penguins *(2005)*
Patience really is a virtue of the observational documentary maker; here a cameraman patiently waits for his talent to get on marching.

> > > **Assignment 2**   ●

Make a list of five subjects or events that would easily lend themselves to an observational documentary.

For example:
Koyaanisqatsi (Life Out of Balance, 1982), *is a good example of an observational documentary. With no conventional plot, it consists of expertly photographed ecology-themed imagery accompanied only by music.*

Participatory type

In a participatory documentary the filmmaker becomes an integral part of the film and appears on-screen. As with the expository documentary, the purpose is to present an argument, only this time it's directly presented to the viewer via the "host" of the program. The person or "star" who is addressing the camera and viewer directly is the catalyst from which the documentary forms. Prime examples are Michael Moore in *Bowling For Columbine*, which addresses the overzealousness of gun ownership in the U.S., and Morgan Spurlock who, in *Super Size Me*, ate nothing but McDonald's fast food for a month. These two documentary makers present themselves as the American "everyman."

Participatory documentaries are sometimes as much about the on-screen filmmaker as they are about the subject matter; thus participatory is also expository. Also, the host's personality is part of the "draw" for the viewer, which means that we are getting much more of a biased perspective on the topic and subject matter, since everything is being filtered through this personality. Because we are primarily dealing with a quirky individual, many of these types of documentaries have a high entertainment value and therefore are more likely to be released theatrically.

A participatory style is commonly used for nature television programs, such as *The Jeff Corwin Experience* and *Crocodile Hunter*, in which the expert talks about and interacts with the animals. The expert also supplies the show's entertainment value.

REALITY TV

• *Reality TV features unscripted real events, humorous or dramatic, with actual people rather than actors. People are placed in situations in which they have to react, such as on a tropical island or stuck in a house with ten other strangers to see how they will interact with one another. The viewer gets entertainment from this.*

• *The appeal for television producers is that it is relatively cheap and quick to produce. Recently, a series of "reality-type" programs with historical significance aired on PBS. In both* Frontier House *and* 1940s House *a group of people were observed while trying to live as their predecessors did. As they discovered the hardships and even talked to the camera about their difficulties adapting, they conveyed to the viewer how people lived during that specific time.*

• *Other examples of reality TV include* Candid Camera, Survivor, Big Brother, *and* Fear Factor. *Reality programs such as these use aspects of all four documentary types.*

● >>> Assignment 3

Do you think it would benefit or hinder the documentary if you were the host? Why or why not? If so, what would you best be able to talk about?

● >>> Assignment 4

Make a list of five random documentaries you have seen and determine what type category they best fit into. Note whether they fit two or more of the categories, and if so, why?

For example:
Ken Burns' Civil War *series is a good example of a dramatic documentary. The film uses archival photos coupled with voice-overs from actors, who read quotes of the period from historical figures, such as Abraham Lincoln and Walt Whitman.*

Super Size Me *(2004)*
Director and star Morgan Spurlock gained over 20 lb (10 kg)—and an addiction to fast food—in order to prove the point of his participatory documentary.

Dramatic documentary type

The dramatic documentary deals with actual historical events through various means, such as with stock footage, archival photos, illustrations, and even reenactments. It conveys its information by presenting a dramatic portrayal of a true subject, most often because that true subject no longer exists.

If you are making a documentary about a person who died years ago, you may have photos and video of them, and perhaps interviews with surviving friends and relatives. If it is a subject that is much older, such as the Salem witch trials, where no photos or images exist from the period, it is perfectly acceptable to use reenactments. However, these reenactments are mostly used in conjunction with a voice-over, whether it be that of an expert being interviewed or a narrator. A viewer watching this will understand that they aren't really watching footage from 400 years ago. A graphic may even state "reenactment" at the bottom of the screen to clarify this. Yet, if the

American Splendor (2003)
This "docudrama" about cartoonist Harvey Pekar primarily has an actor in the role but does include interviews with the real person. It is not true or accurate in every detail, since the actors are working from written dialogue scripts.

Touching the Void (2003)
This dramatic documentary combines reenactments and interviews with climbers Richard Hawking and Simon Yates, to tell the harrowing story of their 1985 mountain climb in the Peruvian Andes.

actors in the reenactment are talking to one another (dialogue), this departs from the facts and goes into the realm of "docudrama," which refers to a fictional film based on true events.

Documentaries about dinosaurs, which reenact these extinct creatures' lives through computer animation, based on the evidence of fossilized remains, can also be considered dramatic documentaries.

The goal of a dramatic documentary is to show the viewer a different perspective on a world other than their own. They can also be expository and participatory.

The docudrama

Docudramas and biographical movies are not considered documentaries. While docudramas may emulate documentary style, perhaps by having simulated interviews, they have much more in common with fictional films.

> KEY POINTS: The four types of documentary

1 Expository
> Interactive with the subjects, interviewees are asked questions.
> May or may not have narration.
> Linear flow—in the order in which it happens.
> Strong point of view.

2 Observational
> Non-intervention of filmmaker with subjects.
> No asking questions directly.
> Longer camera takes.
> Synchronous sound—what you see has the actual sound that goes with it.

3 Participatory
> The filmmaker or host is the central catalyst of the documentary.
> Biased opinion/viewpoint, most likely that of the host.
> Higher entertainment value for viewer.

4 Dramatic
> Focus on events as they are known or believed to be true at the time.
> Use of narrative techniques to flesh out the story, such as reenactments.
> Less of the documentary maker's point of view.

Lesson 2 : Choosing a subject

Your documentary can be on any subject. There have been documentaries on everything from the migration of lemmings in the Arctic to the establishment of World Peace Day at the United Nations. It can even be on a specific person or on how to do something. The possibilities are limitless, and deciding what to tackle can be difficult.

> > > Assignment 5

Make a list of ten subjects that are within driving distance of where you live and that will lend themselves to a documentary. Include a sentence or two establishing why you think each topic would be interesting for a viewer.

It is a good idea to pick a topic that you are familiar with or have a keen interest in, but it must also be a subject that you have access to and can tackle with your resources. If you live in Iowa and have a limited budget, doing a documentary on elephants in Africa probably isn't realistic. However, if you have a huge budget, make sure you enjoy the savanna while shooting the pachyderms.

You may not even have to look very far to find your subject. Keep your eyes and ears open and look at things more closely. Ultimately, the most important thing is that the subject you choose is interesting to you, since you will be living with the project for months, or even years.

Avoid the obvious

You will want to avoid subjects that have been done before, such as people struggling with addictions or pollution. These may be popular topics, but the chances are distributors will pass on your project because they already have a dozen programs on that same subject. If, for some reason, you do decide to undertake something that has been done before, make sure you put your own spin on it, to set it apart from the others. For example, you may choose to do a documentary on "the homeless and their pets," which is a new slant on an old topic.

Consider the viewer

Another factor that may determine what you choose as your subject is who your audience is. Are you making this for yourself and your friends, or is it intended to inform the masses? Is it an educational documentary, or is it more geared toward entertainment? By determining who your audience is, you can begin to establish your goal for the program. (See also Who is your audience, pages 16–17.)

Sieze every opportunity
If you live next door to an eccentric family who grew the world's largest squash after trying to grow one for 20 years, their story may make for a good documentary, if they are amenable to it.

105 topics that lend themselves to a documentary treatment

1 Public transportation
2 Bottled water
3 Sesame-seed allergies
4 Lifestyle of single fathers
5 Airport security
6 In-home hospice
7 Independent living for the mentally handicapped
8 Special-needs pets
9 Same-sex marriages
10 Affirmative action
11 Health services for the elderly
12 Bilingual education in schools
13 How to save energy costs
14 Cost of health care
15 Having a child at a later age
16 Reparations for slavery
17 What it means to be an immigrant
18 The effects of video games on teenagers
19 People for sale
20 Ebay addiction
21 Sweatshop-free clothing
22 Ostrich farming
23 Innate behavior in humans
24 Honeybee navigation
25 Bioluminescence
26 People who work night shifts
27 Cancer immunotherapy
28 Ecosystem of the backyard
29 Sewage treament
30 Pitbull rescue
31 Evolution and adaptation
32 Birth control
33 Human cloning

34 Prenatal screening scares
35 Moss life cycle
36 Why does Gothic subculture have a bad reputation?
37 Emancipated minors
38 "Pushy parent" syndrome
39 Death and dying
40 Insurance for pets
41 How to not look like a tourist
42 Caregivers
43 Growing gardens in the city
44 Pet euthanasia
45 Germans who lived through World War II
46 American saints
47 Abducted reporters
48 Genes behind severe arthritis
49 The causes of deformed frog populations
50 Caffeine addiction
51 Graffiti artists
52 Gypsies in the twenty-first century
53 The disappearance of the middle class
54 The meaning of dreams
55 Training miniature horses to assist the blind
56 Modern-day cowboys
57 The digital revolution
58 Science-fiction conventions
59 National crime prevention
60 Gas prices
61 The history of body piercing
62 Aboriginal spirituality
63 Intelligence and the brain
64 Paganism in the modern world
65 How meditation affects illness
66 Eco-spirituality and living with the Earth
67 Nanotechnology
68 Subjective reality
69 What is transhumanism?
70 Mayans today
71 Adrenaline junkies
72 Aging and memory
73 Is there such a thing as altruism?
74 Anxiety disorders

75 Artificial creativity
76 Automatic behavior
77 Behavior modification
78 Near-death experiences
79 American belief systems
80 Body language
81 Weight gain in the Midwest
82 Behavior disorders
83 The history of plumbing
84 Are twins really similar?
85 How color affects behavior
86 Communism
87 Conformity
88 Exotic pets
89 People living in the wild
90 Unusual careers
91 Animal self-awareness
92 Speed reading
93 Stereotypes
94 Chinese mathematics
95 Forgery
96 The modern zoo
97 The size of the universe
98 Frog calls
99 "The girl next door"
100 Children and technology
101 Deadly blood disorders
102 The stigma of suicide
103 Twenty-first century Goths
104 The fear spread by television news
105 Shaken baby syndrome

Subjects to avoid

1 **The health risks of fast food.**
This topic already had high-profile coverage in *Super Size Me* and is always in the news.

2 **The health care crisis in the U.S.**
A subject that has been overdone in the media and effectively covered by Michael Moore in *Sicko*.

3 **Animal Welfare.**
Animal Planet channel and organizations such as PETA have this area well covered.

4 **The war in Iraq.**
Since there is so much media coverage, and many documentaries have been made on this subject, it is too familiar to the general public.

5 **The homeless.**
This is usually one of the first ideas that comes to the mind of someone just beginning in documentary making, especially if they are interested in social documentaries.

Lesson 3 :
Who is your audience?

The goal of your documentary is to reach as wide an audience as possible. Once you have decided on the subject for the documentary, the next important step is to determine your eventual audience. Who is going to watch it? Who do you want it to reach? And, more specifically, why are they going to watch it?

> Objectives

> To decide on your intended audience—who is going to be viewing your program?

> To determine the "watchability" of the chosen subject.

If you are making a program on how the increase in diabetes will affect future health care, is your audience the "general population," with the hope of spreading awareness and perhaps instigating social reform? Or is the aim simply to educate people about the subject matter?

The key is to make your program interesting to the viewer; therefore you must have some idea of who that viewer will be. After all, there are over six billion people in the world, so there is an audience for any topic or subject. Yet you need to narrow this down in order to begin to plan your specific documentary.

● >>> Assignment 6

Write down five topics you are interested in pursuing, then make a list of who you believe will want to watch that program.

Your demographics
Think about your target audience. What is their age, sex, education, economic status, and their political, cultural, and religious beliefs?

Find your average audience

In order to find out who your audience is and tailor a documentary to suit them, consider each of the key points called out to the right. You really need to take the time to think about who you are talking to and what their level of understanding is. Are they under 12 years old? Are they over 60? What are the cultural taboos of the country you are shooting in?

If the primary purpose of the documentary is to teach about a certain health condition, such as dyslexia, then your audience may be those affected by it, as well as their extended family and friends. This would make your audience children as well as adults, and the film may even be used as a teaching tool in schools and libraries. If you are making the program in English, then the much larger audience is the Western world.

If you are making a movie about the Church of Satan and expect it to be a hit in the U.S.'s Bible Belt region, you will be sorely disappointed. However, if you are seeking to be controversial, make it for a niche adult audience who enjoys alternative viewpoints, or for the festival circuit (see pages 128–129).

You need to know your audience before you start planning your documentary, because depending on all of the above, you will need to adjust your message and information to meet or exceed their expectations.

KEY POINTS: Aspects of your audience to consider

> Age
> Sex
> Education
> Culture
> Politics
> Religion
> Health

MARKET FORCES

● *Who your intended audience is will also affect how you go about producing the documentary. Where do you intend to show it? How is it going to reach your target audience?*

● *While the documentary may be made with a specific audience in mind, it also has to appeal to the market. Is this a program that you will send to festivals in the hope of knocking the socks off the judges? Is it a program suitable for PBS? Or is it something you will sell yourself on the Internet?*

Lesson 4 : Do your research

Once you have determined what your subject is and who your audience is, it is time to gather your information so that you can ultimately present it in an interesting way. Your research begins with asking questions and becoming familiar with your subject matter. It is your ultimate job to become an expert on it.

› Objective

> To become as familiar with your subject matter as is possible and to enable you to produce a documentary rich in information and of interest to your audience.

KEY POINTS:
Investigating your topic

> Collect data from books and the Internet.

> Talk to experts on the subject.

> Analyze all the information gathered and decide what the best information is.

> Decide the scope of the production.

> Will the film have credibility?

> Is your information representative of your topic?

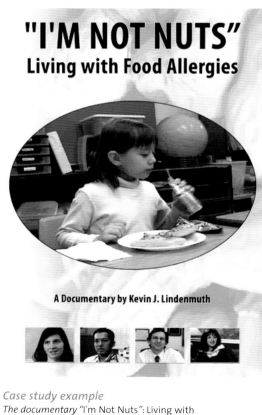

Case study example
The documentary "I'm Not Nuts": Living with Food Allergies (2009) is used to exemplify the teaching points in this article. The focus of this program is on children, since it is normally during childhood that a person is diagnosed with a food allergy. The coping and managing of the allergies is revealed through a series of "why?" questions answered by parents and allergists.

What needs to be said?

First of all, you need to ascertain what level of information you will convey to your audience. Is it for a novice, someone who knows little or nothing about the subject matter, or for someone who is already familiar with the topic? Will you be providing concrete information in the form of figures and facts, or will your documentary consist of a series of interviews and attempt to evoke a much more philosophical or emotive response to interviewees' personal opinions or experiences? Read around your subject as much as possible. If you yourself are well informed about the subject, you'll be in a good position to present the necessary information to your intended audience in the best possible way.

Take the documentary "*I'm Not Nuts*": *Living with Food Allergies* (2009), for example. This will be watched by those directly affected by food allergies, as well as their extended friends and families, from adolescents to grandparents. It is a teaching tool suitable for schools and libraries that a viewer would seek out, rather than casually watch for strictly entertainment value. It also speaks directly to those food-allergic families, who are considered the "experts" because they live with the condition on a daily basis, and is a film that allergy doctors can recommend to their patients. While some information provided is probably already familiar to those who deal with the problem on a daily basis, there is new information to those who are learning about the dangers for the first time. Therefore, it is intended for the widest audience possible.

Get your facts straight

All documentaries intend to be informative, so to ensure that your program fulfills this aim, you should look to provide as much concrete and reliable information as you can. Your research involves gathering true facts, reading books written by experts, and perusing the Web. As the documentary maker, you must take this information and decide what the most important aspects are to convey to the viewer, and what needs to be shown and talked about first. Writing down important aspects, theories, and points of view on the subject is a good idea. This is the information that must be conveyed.

In the case of the food allergy documentary, statistics and scientific fact come into play, answering basic questions such as, "How many people actually have food allergies in the United States and worldwide?," "Is there a difference from country to country?," "Do people understand it is a dangerous condition?," and "What are the common misconceptions about the condition?" By researching the subject, reading books by noted physicians, and perusing support websites, it's ascertained that important aspects to convey to the viewer are theories as to why allergies are increasing, what the top eight allergens are, and the understanding of what happens to the body when an allergen is ingested. This is the information that must be conveyed in your documentary movie.

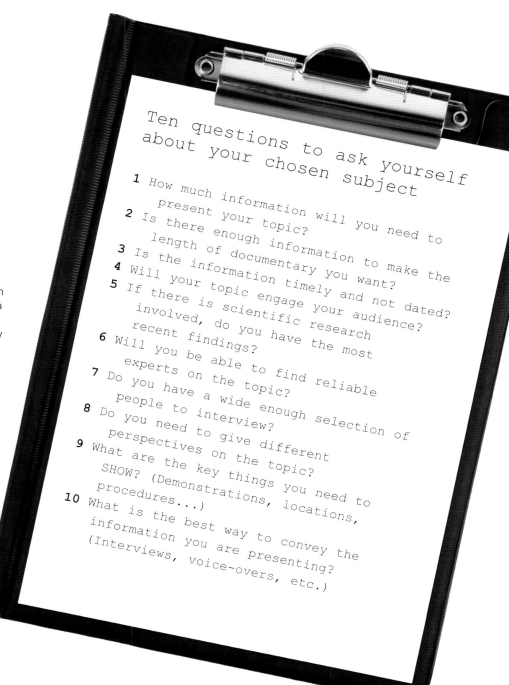

Ten questions to ask yourself about your chosen subject

1 How much information will you need to present your topic?

2 Is there enough information to make the length of documentary you want?

3 Is the information timely and not dated?

4 Will your topic engage your audience?

5 If there is scientific research involved, do you have the most recent findings?

6 Will you be able to find reliable experts on the topic?

7 Do you have a wide enough selection of people to interview?

8 Do you need to give different perspectives on the topic?

9 What are the key things you need to SHOW? (Demonstrations, locations, procedures...)

10 What is the best way to convey the information you are presenting? (Interviews, voice-overs, etc.)

● >>> **Assignment 7**

Choose a topic and, before you do any research, make a list of ten questions that you immediately have about it.

Interviews

After gathering all the information and defining the common threads, it is time to make a list of questions based on the information you have uncovered. In the case of the allergy film, some of the questions will be intended for the allergy doctors, other questions for the families dealing with food allergies, and others directly for the kids and adults who actually have the allergies. For example, the questions asked of the doctors will deal with researched facts and statistics. Questions for the families will be about personal experience and will all be similar, though some may differ depending on the unique circumstances of the interviewee—such as having a newborn sufferer or a teenager. Many people will be asked the same questions because they will probably answer them differently, based on their own experiences.

Next it is time to find individuals who will answer these questions honestly and give the documentary credibility. After all, you are not only researching your information, you are researching the best people to interview. Finding suitable people to interview (who will really bring something to your movie) is an important part of your documentary research.

There is also the matter of scope to consider. Will everything be shot locally, or is there travel involved? There are certain factors that may determine this, such as budget and resources. The scope will immediately narrow or widen your options for gathering people to interview.

Get a good mix
If your documentary is about a widespread topic, such as food allergies, it is best to have a good variety of ages and ethnicities represented, especially if the program is for PBS. On the right is a cross-section of the interviewees who appeared in the "I'm Not Nuts": Living With Food Allergies documentary. It consists of: the children (1, 2, 4, and 5) who are directly affected by the allergies; the parents (1 and 4) who are coping with the allergy and its consequences; and the experts (3 and 6)—the doctors, health care professionals, and support groups who provide specialist knowledge and give the topic (and your documentary) credibility.

Tip

Be prepared to adjust
Bear in mind that, although you have an initial idea of what your documentary is going to be about, as you carry out your research you may decide against that choice, or be drawn to a different aspect than originally intended. Your ideas may even change and become refined or expanded as your research progresses.

TECHNIQUE FILE

Find your interviewees

To get the best interviewees, there are several key things to do:

1 Prepare a persuasive pitch: You'll need to "sell" your documentary to those who you want to recruit. It's important to be informative but concise—you don't want to bore the target before they get to the end!

2 Contact people far ahead of time: Good interviewees are worth their weight in gold.

3 E-mail far and wide: Contact as many potential interviewees as you can. You are likely to receive more responses and have a greater pool from which to choose.

4 Bag the experts: These are the most important interviewees, so get them first. They are the substance of the program and supply the majority of the concrete facts.

5 Meet the interviewees in person: It's important to see how they look and talk prior to filming. Documentaries are a visual medium and very little can be told of a person from the written word or a static photo. It is vitally important that these individuals come off well on camera. When you first meet them, bring a camera and tape a few minutes of them speaking.

Example pitch
This pitch was sent out to find interviewees for the allergy documentary, "I'm Not Nuts": Living with Food Allergies. It was e-mailed to local food allergy support groups, clinics, and a few national support groups, who were able to recommend known specialists in the area. Responses were received from several doctors, who had heard about it through the food allergy support groups they consult for, and they were in turn able to recommend families (covering a wide age-range) suitable for interviewing. One of the doctors has a food-allergic daughter, so was also able to give a personal perspective.

Be sure to introduce yourself and your documentary (specifying where it will be shown, i.e., television, DVD, festivals, etc.).

Give details of your previous credits. Sell yourself!

Include a deadline.

Don't forget to include your contact detail, as part of the letterhead or your sign-off.

Provide further information—give the reader the option to delve deeper, if they wish.

Hello. My name is Kevin Lindenmuth. I am producing a new documentary entitled "I'm Not Nuts": Living with Food Allergies, which will be broadcast on PBS. I am seeking to interview someone in your organization, and also parents and children whose daily lives are affected by food allergies.

To tell you briefly about myself, I have produced six previous documentaries, two of which were on multiple sclerosis, and five of which were broadcast on PBS. I am an independent producer/director in Brighton, Michigan, who has completed over a dozen independent features and published two books.

Please let me know as soon as possible if anyone within your organization is interested in being interviewed for the documentary—I hope to have the entire project shot by April 2007. With my previous documentary, I interviewed the vice-president of the National MS Society, Michigan, and included a segment on that organization. Similarly, this documentary could provide great publicity for the organization and raise awareness of the work you do.

Pasted below (and attached) is further information on the project, together with links to my previous work.

I look forward to hearing from you soon.

K. J. Lindenmuth

Preparing interview questions

The questions you ask your interviewees are designed to supply the substance of your documentary, so it's important for you to get them right. Take time to think about:

1 The number: It's a good rule of thumb to have at least eight questions but no more than 15, as you don't want to overwhelm the interviewee.
2 The style: Your questions need to be straightforward and simply worded. This is especially important if you want the person to integrate the question back into their answer, to give it context.
3 The order: Your questions should run in a logical order. For example, if it's a documentary about training a guide dog, the first questions should elicit information about training the dog as a puppy.
4 Repetition: Some of your questions might need to be repeated with different people so you have the option of choosing the best answers/ information during editing.
5 Tailoring questions: Some questions will need to be tailored specifically to the individual. Keep in mind that new questions may arise spontaneously during the interview. If you think a tangent is worth pursuing, go with your gut, as long as you get your primary information.

Opposite are the interview questions formulated for the food allergy documentary. Compare those written for the families with those tailored to the experts.

Questions for families

Although many of the questions will be similar, there are always a few that are specific to the individual, based on the initial conversations.

1   How did you get your allergy?
2   What did your doctor tell you about allergies?
3   What do you have to do to make sure you and your daughter don't come into contact with those foods? What precautions do you have to take?
4   How do other people react to the allergies? Is there any frustration from people who don't have allergies, or who have difficulty understanding the seriousness of the allergy, that it's life-threatening?
5   How has this affected you (from not having this allergy from before you were pregnant), and how do you think it will affect your daughter?
6   What helps you cope with the allergies?
7   Will you have more children, knowing there's a good chance they will have food allergies?
8   Can you tell us about the support you have received from support groups and other resources?

Questions for doctors

The doctor here was asked many of the same questions as the other two doctors, but a few were specific, since he had recently been involved with research on a particular aspect.

1   Can people be allergic to any food? And why are they allergic to a food?
2   How does a person's body react to a food allergy?
3   What causes food allergies? Is it environmental or hereditary?
4   When a mother is pregnant or is breastfeeding, does what she is eating influence whether or not her child will develop a food allergy?
5   What are common misconceptions about food allergies?
6   Are food allergies increasing in the U.S. and worldwide, or are we just better at identifying them?
7   Why do you think there is a less serious response to food allergies than to, let's say, a bee allergy?
8   In your experience, what is the first reaction parents have when you tell them their child has a food allergy? Do a lot of parents worry that their child won't have a "normal" life?
9   What do you tell them that helps to ease the news or put it in a perspective they can deal with?

Drafting a synopsis

At this point in your research, after finding all the relevant information to convey and people to interview, you should decide on your focus and content by writing a description of the program.

An example of a focus and content synopsis might take the following form:

> Concisely list the key points you will address in the documentary.

> Choose a catchy, memorable title for your project.

"I'm Not Nuts":
Living with Food Allergies

Focus

The purpose of this documentary is to improve the awareness of the general public as to how serious these food allergies can be, clear up misinformation people commonly have about food allergies, and, most importantly, show that this is something you can live with. It will also provide additional resources for support and education.

Content

This program will view both the personal and professional perspectives. The 85-minute documentary will focus on several families in the Midwest as well as information from medical experts. There will be children with food allergies as well as adults.

With the children, the focus is primarily on how the parents have dealt with the allergies and what they do to minimize them. On the one hand, the parents have to "normalize" the situation with the allergic children, but at the same time they have to convey the gravity of the situation to extended family members (ie, grandparents) and others they and their children interact with.

The film will address the following issues:

* The impact on the parents', child's, and siblings' daily routine
* Educating children and other family members about preventing a reaction
* The time and energy that goes into preparing for eating out, going to the park, visiting family and friends
* Dealing with daycare/school/public
* Lack of understanding or education among family members who are unaware of or misinformed about the condition

Several medical professionals will talk about the specifics of what happens with an allergic reaction, why allergies occur and what to do about them, and what the future holds in terms of prevention and possible cure.

The various coping challenges and strategies—medical, emotional, and social—will be addressed by the documentary.

The in-depth struggles of the individual and their family will be portrayed. The positive lessons gained from learning to cope with allergies effectively on a daily basis will also be shown.

> Summarize, in no more than two paragraphs, what the documentary is about. Make it interesting!

Lesson 5 : Choosing a style

Once you have chosen your topic, it is time to determine the particular style that will suit it best. The most important thing is that the style complements the chosen topic and message of the documentary.

Objective

> To determine which particular style is best suited for your project.

Shoot and edit

"Style" refers to the aesthetic or design of the program. This is how ideas, images, and sounds are expressed and shown to the viewer. A documentary's particular style is established through both the shooting and editing. They are both equally important. For example, if the documentary is about a group of graffiti artists in Detroit who have to dodge the law in order to create their art, the style could include handheld, "shaky" camera interviews, quick edits, and time-lapse to show the rapid creation of a graffiti mural. Likewise, if an individual is talking about coping with depression, then the use of nature shots—such as a foggy or rainy day—that emphasize the emotions being discussed would be more relevant.

Similarly, one documentary may consist of solely archival photos and footage, while another chooses to show everything through faithful reenactments. The style is also created by how you shoot the documentary, through framing and angles. Do your interviews consist primarily of wide shots or close-ups? Are there moving shots, or is everything still and shot from a tripod? Is natural lighting used, or do you need a truckload of lighting equipment to get the mood you want?

While there is nothing wrong with emulating the shooting and editing of your favorite documentaries, you will discover that your own documentary's style is very much influenced by your own preferences. Remember, there are really no "set" categories for documentary style.

Comparing styles
Here are examples of stills from two documentaries that differ in how they are shot. What they do have in common, though, is that they both use natural lighting. The graffiti sequence (stills 1–4, top) is shot with a handheld camera, and begins outside of the old abandoned building, showing all the graffiti, then "walks" inside to show more within. The jerky nature of the filming matches the edgy subject matter. The other documentary (stills 1–4, below) consists of a series of tripod shots of sundown on a summer day. The stillness of the subject is matched by the steadily held camera.

DEVELOPING A STORY ARC

Whatever subject you choose as the focus for your documentary, it will need to tell a story. This should follow that of a fictional narrative film, with a beginning, middle, and end—a story arc that draws the viewer in, makes them respond to your program, and takes them along for the ride. Your story will also determine your program's structure (see page 102) and influence your overall blueprint (see page 36). Whatever your subject or unfolding theme is, it's important that your film has a story arc. Remember that whatever drew you to your

documentary subject to begin with was most likely the potential story. Stay committed to it!

For a scripted documentary, the script itself will aid the creation of the story. The characters will be introduced, their obstacle/cause will be presented, and then it will be resolved (or not). For example, you may be making a program on a rock and roll band whose lead singer has Tourette's syndrome. Through the script, the documentary will first present his problem and then develop

the story on how he works around his condition, before ending on how he makes the condition work for him. This is the arc.

A program that interviews dozens of people who witnessed the falling of the Twin Towers on 9/11 will also have its own story arc. Each of the interviewees will have their own specific stories, but the overall show will have a broader story arc—that of society coping with this disaster.

Direct cinema

The broadest documentary style is often referred to as *cinéma vérité*, or "direct cinema." This term was coined to identify documentaries in which a person or group is followed and their reactions are captured on film, as in an observational documentary. However, this has become such a standard that it can refer to virtually any documentary that is not a reenactment or made from archival material.

Cinéma vérité

This sequence of stills from a documentary about living with allergies shows a boy helping his mother make raspberry cake using ingredients that he is not allergic to. The camera remains unobtrusive, capturing the interaction as it happens. It is then edited together in the order in which it happened.

DEALING WITH POLITICS

The way in which politics affects your documentary can become apparent at any point in the process. At the beginning of the production, for example, you may run into difficulties when finding experts on your subject. Let's say you are doing a program on Florida manatees and approach two different naturalists, both of whom would be invaluable. However, you soon find out that one of them refuses to be in the film if the other is included, either due to rivalry or bad blood between them, never mind that the program has nothing to do with this. You must pick the best expert, which would probably be the one who did not make the fuss.

Alternatively, you may be working on a profile piece looking at how several people and their families are coping with various diagnoses of cancer. It is intended as an informational program to help other families in the same situation. You have the full cooperation of a national cancer support center and are given open doors and fantastic cooperation from their staff and patients. However, when the documentary is completed, this same organization will not have anything to do with it, because it does not represent their "mission statement." This may take you completely by surprise, since it is not at all what you intended and, in fact, you were hoping they'd help spread the word about the film.

These examples illustrate why the decisions you make for your documentary must always come back to you, and not be made by a committee. Your goal may be to make the most family-friendly program about the origin of the teddy bear, but rest assured, it's going to offend someone. So don't worry about what everyone else may be thinking, and make the documentary you would like to watch.

The "fake documentary" or "mockumentary": Fiction films shot in documentary style

The term "documentary style" is applied to fictional films that make it seem as if a documentary is being shot, handheld, and is reporting what is actually happening in the narrative. Lately, this is a favorite style of horror films, from *The Blair Witch Project* (1999) and *Quarantine* (2008) to *Cloverfield* (2008) and *Paranormal Activity*. This is a way for the filmmakers to make it seem more real to the audience, although it is an entirely fabricated story.

The art of illusion
While it may look like the "filmmaker" simply picked up a camera and started shooting, these fiction films are meticulously planned and often use state-of-the-art special effects in order to make the action seem real.

>>> Assignment 8

Make a list of how your overall documentary will be shot and edited and what you hope to achieve by doing it this way. Is it because of the audience, or do you simply think it would be interesting, or both?

Lesson 6 : **Scripted vs. unscripted**

Whether a documentary is scripted or unscripted depends on several aspects that hinge on your style as a director/producer, on the subject matter, and also on the type of documentary you are making.

> **Objective**
> To determine whether your documentary needs to be scripted or not. What are the benefits and disadvantages of each way? What will work best to communicate your information?

Key characteristics of a scripted documentary

> Very specific.
> More planning is required when shooting.
> Determines editing.

Scripted

The script details the entire documentary: what is shot, the specific images, any specific effects for transitions from one scene to another, the length of an interview and generally what the interviewee will say, and the narration, if there is any. A scripted documentary will also determine much of the shooting and editing, since the footage will follow the written script.

The majority of scripted documentaries are about something that has already happened, such as an event in history or the life of a person. A scripted documentary may even be based on a nonfiction book, such as Irwin Allen's 1952 Academy Award-winning documentary, *The Sea Around Us* based on a book by Rachel Carson. Even speculative documentaries, such as *The World Without Us*, which hypothesizes about what will happen if humans disappeared from the face of the Earth, are scripted. As such, these documentaries usually entail much more research on the part of the filmmaker. A scripted participatory documentary may also be a true story that unfolds, such as a quest for answers, or a mystery that's ultimately solved in some manner.

The limitations of the script
In a scripted documentary based around interviews, often you can only write the questions you ask your interviewee. After all, you want their answers to be their own.

WHAT TO WATCH

The Undertaking (2007) is a great example of a scripted documentary, as it is based on a nonfiction book by poet and undertaker Thomas Lynch. The hour-long program only covers a fraction of the original material, but documentaries based on books are almost always scripted.

DOES IT SOUND NATURAL?

● *Keep in mind that writing dialogue that someone speaks out loud is different than writing something that someone will only read to themselves.*
● *When writing your script, make sure you frequently read it aloud, and aim to make it sound natural, not something that someone is reading.*

Unscripted

The only type of documentary that could not be scripted is an observational documentary. An unscripted style lends itself to films that document something that is currently happening, where the outcome and footage content is largely unknown beforehand. An unscripted documentary would have just an outline, and perhaps questions that people are being asked.

You know the gist of what people are going to say and what information you are going to cover, but not in exact detail. The documentary is then edited to who gave the best information/ answers. Overall, unscripted documentaries have a much more organic approach. They develop and take shape as you are working on them, so the filmmaking is a process of discovery.

Key characteristics of an unscripted documentary

> May have a guide/blueprint.
> Knows what it wants to get across but will not achieve this until footage is shot and edited.
> More work in editing and selecting footage.
> More spontaneous.

● > > > Assignment 9

Make a list of the reasons why your documentary should be scripted, and then the reasons why it should not. What is the best format for your film?

COMPARE AND CONTRAST

Below a snippet of a documentary about turtles— Shelling out for turtles—is shown in both scripted and unscripted format.

Note: Both the scripted and the unscripted versions may indeed have many of the same visuals, but the scripted format is much more specific. Because you don't know exactly what's going to be said in the unscripted format, the visuals aren't decided until the editing process. With the scripted format, it's just a matter of making a list and shooting everything that is described in the script.

Whether it is scripted or unscripted, many of the same shots will be used. The four shots shown below fit question 2 of the unscripted documentary, and also fit the scripted documentary, with the narrator's opening paragraph.

Unscripted—Shelling out for turtles

Questions for the "expert," such as a herpetologist or a veterinarian.

1 How long have turtles been around?

2 How many different species are kept as pets?

3 What do you think the appeal is of having a turtle as a pet?

4 How long can a pet turtle live in captivity?

Scripted—Shelling out for turtles

Narrator: Turtles, which are often kept as a popular pet, date back to 215 million years ago and are a more ancient group than both snakes and lizards. They have remained relatively unchanged, just like sharks and cockroaches, which means they are well adapted to their environment. There are around 300 different species, of all different sizes, that live on land and water.

[visuals: various shots of different pet turtles and their enclosures]

Narrator: Unlike a cat or a dog, some turtles can live to 150 years, so it takes a bit of devotion. But what, exactly, is the appeal of these ancient creatures to their owners?

[visuals: shot of cat/dog, more shots of turtles]

Lesson 7 : **Narration vs. no narration**

The narration of a documentary must communicate the story without getting in the way, and whether or not you need narration depends on the specifics of the documentary you are making.

> **Objective**

> To decide whether you need narration in your documentary. What will it bring to your film? Is it simply to introduce the subject or is it a presence throughout and the "voice" of the program?

Narration

Narration is primarily used in scripted documentaries in which you have lots of facts and information to get across to the viewer. For example, the style of many nature documentaries is to have a narrator explain what is happening on-screen. Narration can also add a sense of drama to the proceedings. Historical documentaries rely on the narration to convey information and make the facts more compelling. Having narration in a biographical documentary can make the viewer relate more to the person being talked about. Narration may also be a necessity, especially if you have a limited amount of time to convey information about a subject. In fact, even unscripted documentaries may have introductory narration to establish the premise of the program. If you need to quickly convey information at the beginning of a program, it's probably best to use narration.

Narration is also a powerful tool. Because the narrator is directly telling the viewer something, they exert more influence than if the viewer were simply watching the visuals. This is why narration is a staple of the expository documentary.

Narrators can also bring a certain extra element with them, particularly if they are a well-known celebrity. Would it be more effective to have an unknown narrator voice a documentary about Mars, or would it be better to have someone like Patrick Stewart? When you make the choice of a narrator you have to take into account what type of voice will best fit. Do they have a harsh voice or a warm voice? Do you need a man or a woman to do the voice-over? Do you need someone with an English accent, and if so, what type of English accent?

No narration

A documentary does not have to include narration. Telling a story through interviews and footage can work just as well, depending on the "feel" of the program. There is also the option of using visual text, perhaps to explain something at the beginning of the documentary, or as chapter markers—perhaps in the form of a question that is then answered by the various interviewees. Visual text is not as intrusive as having an omniscient voice-over, and can be an effective alternative.

Walking with Dinosaurs *(1999)*
Since dinosaurs cannot talk, never mind that they died over 65 million years ago, programs about these creatures obviously need narration.

WHAT TO WATCH

The series *Walking with Dinosaurs* (1999) was narrated by Kenneth Branagh, an established actor known for his Shakespearean roles. However, the same footage used in the kid-oriented *Prehistoric Planet* (2002), narrated by Ben Stiller— known for his Hollywood comedies—gives the program a very different feel. Compare the two.

Autism is a World (2004) The woman narrator is reading what the main character, an autistic woman, has written because she is unable to speak well. The narration is her words but not her voice. This is an example of a very powerful use of narration, because what she says is at odds with how she physically appears.

IF THE VOICE FITS

● When using narration, make sure the voice fits the subject matter. If the documentary is about the lack of clean water in Mexico, you need to ensure that the voice-over is appropriate. A comedic voice, for example, would not be fitting for such a serious subject.

● Like casting an actor for a role, casting a narrator is a specific skill that, if possible, should be left to someone with years of practice. However, if you do not have that experience at your disposal, try finding a voice talent at your local radio stations or at college campus television and radio classes.

THE DIFFERENCE BETWEEN FIRST-, SECOND-, AND THIRD-PERSON NARRATION

FIRST PERSON brings the viewer into the storyteller's experience and adds the storyteller as a character of the documentary:

"I am going to ask him."

SECOND PERSON is more directly addressing the viewer—"telling" them what they will be seeing and what information they are being presented with (commonly used in nature documentaries):

"You are going to see the animal in its natural habitat."

THIRD PERSON is any voice outside of the action (generally used in voice-over style narration). It is used in observational documentaries, explaining to the viewer what is happening in the shot:

"She is going back to the beauty salon."

● TECHNIQUE FILE

Two ways of voicing a narration

In this example, the interviewee is talking about his early memories growing up in Nazi Germany and how that has affected him. The interview will begin with stock footage of World War II and of the Hitler Youth (samples shown, right—images 1–3). The last shot (4) is a photograph of the interviewee at four years old playing with a gun. This shot will dissolve to the interviewee in the present day (5), so we can see that over 60 years have elapsed, yet we can still identify him with his past.

First-person narration
"One part of my life during the war I can never forget is the Hitler Youth. It just totally fascinated me and I couldn't wait to join. I was impressed by their uniforms, their marching, by their music, by their patriotic songs, and incredible camaraderie that I saw there. Not having a father and my mother always being gone I kind of felt 'This is my family.'"

Third-person narration
The one part of life during the War he could never forget was the Hitler Youth. It totally fascinated him and he was very keen to join. He was impressed by the uniforms, the marching, and music, the patriotic songs, and the sense of camaraderie. Since his father had left and his mother was always away, he felt the youth group was like a new family.

Images 1–3: Some stock image websites are free or relatively cheap to use, if you are planning a montage of stills. Many picture libraries also carry archival footage you can draw on.

Take a section of your own documentary and write the narration for this extract from both a first- and third-person standpoint, as above. Taking the subject and intended audience into consideration, what do you think will be the most effective?

Lesson 8 : **Visualize it**

An important factor to consider is how the documentary is going to unfold. How do you imagine it will look once it is all done? This decision will influence how you are going to shoot and edit your production, so it is essential to determine as much of this beforehand.

> Objectives

> Have in your mind a fully formed idea of how your documentary will look, sound, and "feel" before you start.
> Develop a vision for the overall "mood" of the program.

Where to begin

Once you have your idea for the documentary, try to picture it in your mind's eye. What were your first thoughts when you came up with your documentary idea? Write down, and even sketch, all of these ideas in a notebook, because you will be expanding upon them as you flesh out the project.

Visualization

When you are videotaping people, do you imagine sit-down, "talking-head" interviews, or will your subjects be "talking and walking" at a specific location? Not only does this determine where you shoot the documentary, it also determines the placement and use of the camera.

Will the majority of the documentary consist of visuals with voice-over narration and contain very few interviews, such as with a historical documentary that consists mostly of photos and old newsreels? And is that narration going to be in the first, second, or third person (see page 31)?

Keep in mind that documentaries are a visual medium, and today's sophisticated viewers are accustomed to seeing many different images within a program. Also, what is shown may be far more powerful than what is said. Let's say you are interviewing a person about the death of their spouse in a tragic, freak accident. What they say may be important to the documentary, but seeing them get emotional and teary-eyed may make it much more compelling.

The filmmaker's viewpoint

How you visualize your documentary also depends on what you are bringing to it as an individual. All of the research, information, and content of the program is going to be filtered through you. For example, if three different people are making a documentary on the same subject, they will all probably visualize the project in a different way, based on their own experiences and biases, and influenced by what they've liked in other documentaries they have seen. You may try to be as objective as possible, but your point of view is unavoidable.

Man on Wire (2008)

A great example of visualization, this movie utilizes recent first-person interviews of wire-walker Philippe Petit and his friends talking about their experience of pulling off a tightwire walk between the Twin Towers in New York, in 1974 without getting caught. These interviews are combined with actual footage they took of the event, which is necessary to make the story all the more visual.

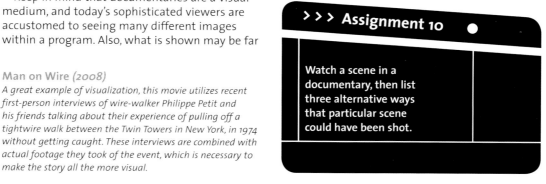

> > > **Assignment 10**

Watch a scene in a documentary, then list three alternative ways that particular scene could have been shot.

TECHNIQUE FILE

Creating a visual outline of a scene

How do you imagine, in your "mind's eye," a particular scene should look? To create a visual outline of a scene you wish to reproduce, you have two options. One is to write down a shot list of everything you want to capture and the way you want it to look. The other is to actually draw what you have in mind. Both are equally valid, so it really is down to personal preference. Keep in mind that you should be flexible in both regards; as you are shooting "real life," staging shots goes along with "re-creations" and "cheating."

This time the documentary subject is based around New York City in the morning. Below, two filmmakers visualize the opening sequence (stills shown right). One lists the opening scenes, the other sketches the scenes in storyboard style.

1 An establishing shot of New York's Central Park, from the top of one of the surrounding buildings.

2–4 Go to series of wide shots in the park; people walking, jogging, riding bikes.

5 Get closer shots of people with their dogs—and through a montage of shots, see that quite a few people who live in the city do own dogs.

6 The last series of shots will be medium shots and close-ups of people interacting with their canine companions.

Written list or rough sketches?
The visual guide (shown above right) gives the same information as the list (left), though the drawings are more useful if you are trying to communicate your "vision" to a cameraman.

Lesson 9 : **Choosing a title**

The title of your documentary is important; after all, it is how your film will be identified by everyone. Your title may even help you garner distribution and move more DVD copies.

> ### Objective
> > To pick a memorable and unique title. Will your chosen title distinguish your program and sell it to viewers?

The National Geographic documentary about a man who chose to live with a pack of wolves for a year is entitled *A Man Among Wolves*. It is very direct and to the point. *The Last Great Ape*, about the recently discovered bonobos in Africa's Congo, is also straightforward. *The Devil and Daniel Johnston*, about a mentally ill musician who has issues with Satan, is a clever play on the title of the movie *The Devil and Daniel Webster*, about a guy who sold his soul to the devil for fame and fortune. It's an ironic title, which fits the content of the documentary.

    The title *Alien From Earth*, a documentary on Nova (a PBS science program), is a bit more enigmatic and exploitative since the viewer doesn't immediately know it's about the discovery of a diminutive prehistoric human. If someone saw that title in a TV listing, they might tune in just to see what it is about. If a documentary is an adaptation of a book, it will often keep the same title in order to be recognizable to its built-in audience.

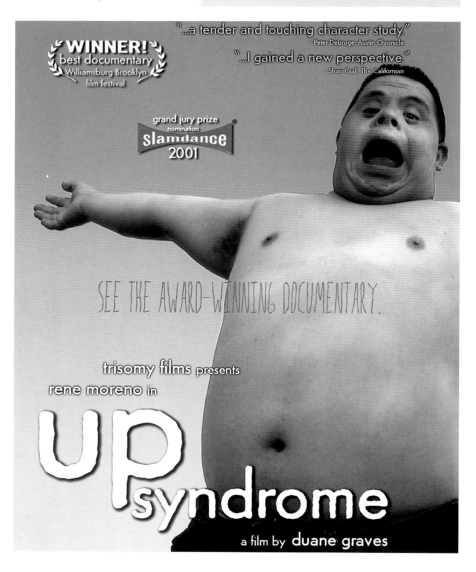

Up Syndrome *(2000)*
Chronicling the filmmaker's charismatic childhood chum who has Down syndrome, the content of this playful, stirring, remarkably unique portrait documentary is captured wonderfully by the title. The substitution of the word "Down" with "Up" presents a much more positive perspective on this chromosomal disorder.

TECHNIQUE FILE

Aim for attention grabbing

● *When choosing a title, start by perusing websites that list documentary films that are similar in topic to your own. A single word or even a phrase could trigger inspiration. Aim to be original and come up with a title that people will remember and that best represents the tone of the program. Don't pick something boring and mundane. You want to get people's attention.*

● *Sometimes a title will come to you right away; at other times it's not until you are editing that you come across a phrase or something that someone says, and you realize it would make a great title.*

● *Before you commit to any titles, first make sure it is not already in use on another production.*

Good titles

Pucker Up: The Fine Art of Whistling *(2005)*
Comical and catchy, this is a perfect and extremely memorable title for a program about one of the most universal musical art forms.

Life in the Freezer *(1993)*
Exploring the natural history of Antarctica, this is an apt but somewhat facetious title for the documentary subject.

In Search Of The Great Beast: Aleister Crowley, The Wickedest Man In The World *(2009)*
This title explains exactly what the documentary is about: a biographical account of the occultist, who referred to himself as "The Great Beast."

The Make-Believers *(2009)*
A feature documentary on computer scams and frauds, this film demonstrates how easy it is to pull off Internet fraud. Filmmaker Glenn Andreiev uses a fabricated website to get people to hand over their identities. While the title doesn't immediately give away the content of the program, it is wonderfully intriguing and suitable for the subject it explores.

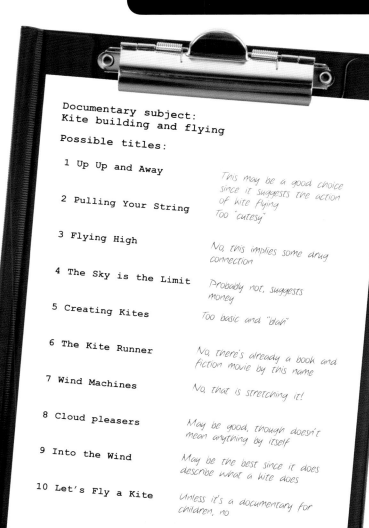

> > > **Assignment 11**

Make a list of ten possible titles for your documentary topic, also listing why each might be a good title. Then pick what you think are the best three and ask friends and family which ones they like best. This will help steer you in the right direction.

Documentary subject:
Kite building and flying

Possible titles:

1 Up Up and Away — *This may be a good choice since it suggests the action of kite flying*

2 Pulling Your String — *Too "cutesy"*

3 Flying High — *No, this implies some drug connection*

4 The Sky is the Limit — *Probably not, suggests money*

5 Creating Kites — *Too basic and "blah"*

6 The Kite Runner — *No, there's already a book and fiction movie by this name*

7 Wind Machines — *No, that is stretching it!*

8 Cloud pleasers — *May be good, though doesn't mean anything by itself*

9 Into the Wind — *May be the best since it does describe what a kite does*

10 Let's Fly a Kite — *Unless it's a documentary for children, no*

Lesson 10 : **Create a blueprint**

Your "blueprint" consists of anything that helps you guide the production of the documentary, whether it is scripted or not.

> **Objective**
> > To gather and select all the written and illustrated materials that will best help you construct the documentary. Will a storyboard help you?

KEY POINTS:
The blueprint checklist

> Script or outline.
> Shot list(s).
> A list of questions to be answered and the points to be covered.
> Storyboard.
> List of everyone involved, from interviewees to production crew.

No generic blueprint exists for making a documentary. Your own particular blueprint should include everything that has helped you organize your film, from notes to questions to what you want to convey to your audience, as well as the visual look you want to capture. It may also include the storyboards (see page 38), a written script, a shot list, use of stock footage, and even music. It is your synopsis, encompassing how much footage you plan to shoot, editing notes, and how you envision transitioning from one scene to another. It details everything that helps you form the documentary before you actually start the production.

Be prepared

Once consolidated, your blueprint may be several pages long or the length of a screenplay, depending on how complicated or involved the production is. For example, a scripted and narrated documentary will have far more prepared information than something that is observational and only capturing a single event. Regardless of its length, think of it as a "skeleton," onto which you successfully build the "meat" of your production. This file will come in handy when you are soliciting and doing interviews and preparing to shoot footage, because you will have many of the answers to questions ahead of time. People will be asking you specific questions about your documentary, so you always need to have a prepared answer.

Remember: Your blueprint will keep you on track and focused during the shooting and editing of the project, but you'll need to be flexible when challenges arise. For example, if you are unable to reschedule an interview, which you planned to shoot outside, you may have to relocate to a nearby building if it's raining.

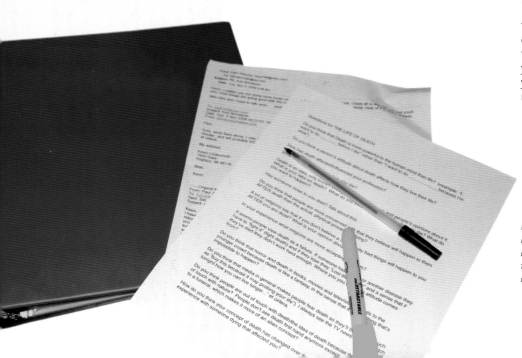

File it
It is a good idea to consolidate all of the associated information and keep it in a three-ring binder so you can refer to it quickly, if needed.

TECHNIQUE FILE

Compiling the shot list

Think of the shot list as your production's "grocery list." It consists of the visuals you need for the documentary. This can be done in many different ways.

- *Plan ahead: If your documentary is scripted, the shot list may already be a part of that script; for instance, it may indicate if you need a shot of a building, inside the lobby of the building, and people working at their desks inside of that building. If this is the case, you may get these shots while you are shooting other scenes at that location. Think about all of the shots you need ahead of time, and build your list accordingly.*
- *Take notes while rolling: In an unscripted documentary, you do not know what shots you need until you tape an interview. You may then find—during shooting or editing—that you need additional footage to tell the story. Jot down the images that come to mind while the documentary is rolling. For example, during an interview scene in which the person is recalling an important childhood event, it may occur to you to use a childhood photo to augment what the person is talking about; or perhaps they even have home movies of themselves at that age. Add these images to the shot list.*
- *Build on your list: During pre-production, a shot list may encompass the entire documentary, especially if it is utilizing archival or stock footage. During production, break the shot list down into specific scenes or interviews. You can then list all the "B-roll" footage (see page 97) you need to shoot while you are there. During post-production, you may have an additional list of new shots that come to mind while you are editing. Make this as simple or as detailed as necessary.*

Allergy documentary:
Additional Shots

1 Subject teaching a teacher group (various shots)

2 Shots of her daughter (whom she mentions)

3 Shots of an elementary school classroom

4 Shots of the epinephrine pen

5 Demonstrating the injection

EXAMPLE SHOT LIST

In this unscripted documentary, a mother explains the importance of knowing how and when to use the "epinephrine pen" on someone who has a severe anaphylactic allergic reaction (to bees, food, and so on). She teaches this information at schools. After the interview with her has been filmed and viewed during editing, a list is made of the shots needed. Compare the list on the left with the corresponding shots taken below. These clips will be cut to during the interview.

The storyboard

The storyboard is a series of images/panels that illustrates how your program's visuals will go together. A storyboard is particularly helpful if you are undertaking a complicated, detail-oriented scene, or one that has action and movement. It is also a benefit if you are going for a certain style or "look" to your documentary.

A storyboard can be created by hand on a sketch pad, or by complicated three-dimensional renderings on a computer. Your storyboard will show how individuals or objects are arranged in a scene, and which direction they will move in. They will also indicate camera movement, the type of shot (close-up, wide shot), the camera angle, and even the transitions that will be used in editing, such as dissolves or jump cuts.

The use of a storyboard is up to the individual filmmaker. Some like to plan everything out ahead of time, as with a scripted documentary, while others are better at, and more creative with, improvising and dealing with situations as they arise.

● >>> **Assignment 12**

Consolidate your blueprint with a shot list and storyboard. What do you find particularly helpful? What is missing?

In the example shown here, John Borowski refines his storyboards for his film *Albert Fish* to include information for the shots. Borowski lists props, costumes, and special makeup effects necessary for filming. He draws his storyboards by hand, then scans them into his Mac where he adds the descriptive information. In shot 3, Borowski utilizes Fish's silhouette from a stock photograph to further assist with his visualization of the final shot for the film.

Your storyboard doesn't have to be a masterpiece! Drawings are a quick and effective way to illustrate the visual elements of your film.

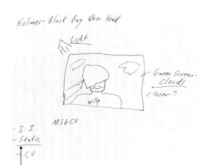

It can be helpful to write notes to accompany your drawings, to expand upon ideas, and to explain any complicated visuals.

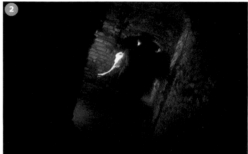

From storyboard to screen

Above are three storyboard and final frames from filmmaker John Borowski's documentary film, H.H. Holmes: America's First Serial Killer (2004). For the production of reenactments, Borowski utilizes sets, miniatures, and green screen. He draws his own storyboards and considers them essential for the production of his films. As much information as possible is put into these drawings, which are accompanied by notes on alternative angles and camera movements for the same shot.

Here, Borowski depicts the protagonist reading a Bible in his jail cell. The director creates atmosphere through clever use of lighting.

ALBERT FISH – Producer/Director: John Borowski – Location: Entertanium Studios

SET: JAIL CELL

SHOT:	FISH READS BIBLE IN JAIL CELL
DESCRIPTION:	FISH SITS HUNCHED OVER READING THE BIBLE WHILE HOLDING A ROSARY. DARK – SHAFTS OF LIGHT – PREFER SILHOUETTE.
TAKES:	WS, MS, TRACKING IN
ACTOR(S):	FISH
COSUTME:	GREY MAN - ?
PROPS:	BIBLE, ROSARY, COT
MAKEUP:	MUSTACHE

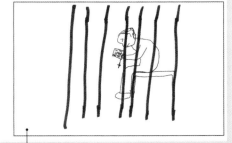

Although a rough rendering, the scene depicted here is a clear visual indicator of the filmed scene (below).

In this scene we are introduced to a young Fish. Using flashbacks in a film is a good way to show how a character might have evolved.

ALBERT FISH – Producer/Director: John Borowski – Location: Entertanium Studios

SET: KEDDEN APARTMENT

SHOT:	KEDDEN WIDE
DESCRIPTION:	KEDDEN SITS ON THE EDGE OF THE BED. YOUNG FISH'S HAND MOVES INTO FRAME HOLDING CAT O' NINE TAILS. WINDOW AS LIGHT SOURCE.
TAKES:	WS STATIC – TRACK IN?
ACTOR(S):	KEDDEN, YOUNG FISH
COSTUME:	KEDDEN COSTUME AND HAT, YOUNG
FISH COSTUME – PAINTER?	
PROPS:	CAT O' NINE TAILS, BED, WHITE SHEET
MAKEUP:	

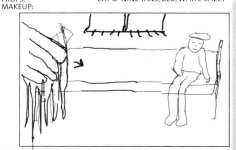

This drawing translates well into the filmed result below.

The director focuses on details like the protagonist staring out of the window of his empty apartment to create a sense of isolation.

ALBERT FISH – Producer/Director: John Borowski

SET: EMPTY APARTMENT

SHOT:	FISH STANDS IN EMPTY APARTMENT
DESCRIPTION:	ZOOM OUT FROM FISH LOOKING OUT WINDOW TO WS EMPTY APARTMENT.
TAKES:	CU & MS FISH AT WINDOW. ZOOM OUT FROM FISH TO WIDE SHOOT END WIDE WITHOUT FISH FOR DISSOLVE.
ACTOR(S):	FISH
COSTUME:	GREY MAN, OVERCOAT, HAT, GREY
SHOES – ALL GREY	
PROPS:	
MAKEUP:	MUSTACHE
LOCATION:	EMPTY APARTMENT

The sketch in this part of the storyboard looks quite different to the filmed result; however it still retains all the key elements of the scene.

EQUIPMENT AND TAPE FORMAT

Making a documentary half a century ago meant shooting on film, an extremely costly process that involved renting the camera equipment, purchasing the film stock, and paying for the processing. Back then equipment was also cumbersome, requiring several people to operate everything, from pulling focus to monitoring the audio. The most nerve-wracking part was that you were not sure how your footage would turn out until you got it back from the film processing lab, which could be weeks or months later. Video was cheaper than film, but it would be decades before it was a readily acceptable format for professional independent productions.

Today, obtaining broadcast-quality video equipment is inexpensive and easy, making it a godsend for the beginner documentary filmmaker. A person can literally go to their local electronics store and buy what they need. However, since there are so many choices, the process of narrowing down the selections and making the initial purchases for a camera, tripod, microphones, and lights can be daunting. The key is to initially buy only what you need to complete the production. Fortunately, while you do need the basics, you do not need nearly as much equipment as you would if you were producing a feature movie. Obtaining the equipment, once difficult, is now one of the easier aspects of documentary production.

DV formats

When deciding on what equipment to purchase, video formats also come into play. Avoid the older analog formats, since these will no longer exist in a few years. All formats are now DV, digital video, whether recorded on physical tapes or on video cards. There is no generational loss with digital media, which means you can copy it a hundred times and the quality will remain the same.

While many of the more expensive documentaries are shot with film, it is much more likely that you will be concerned with the newer digital video formats of SD, "standard definition," and HD, "high definition." In fact, it is somewhat ironic that if you shoot on film nowadays you'll have to transfer all that footage to digital video for editing and distribution.

One of the primary influences on your choice of format will be what you intend to do with the documentary when it is finished. Standard definition, which includes Digi-Betacam, DVCAM, DVCPRO, and MiniDV, is acceptable if you intend to sell DVDs or for television. However, if this is something you might want to show theatrically, HD may be a better choice.

Take your time and do your research when deciding on equipment and format. Ask yourself, "What do I absolutely need to make this project happen?"

CONTENTS / PAGES

Lesson 11 : **Cameras and tripods**

Your choice of camera depends on three things: what you need it to do, where you ultimately want to show your film, and what you can afford or already have access to. This choice can vastly affect the shape of your documentary. If you get a poor image, it's more likely the fault of the camera than the tape format you are shooting on. For this reason, avoid the cheaper consumer cameras.

Production basics
The three most important components of your production are the camera, tripod, and lights.

Tape or hard drive?

If you have a limited budget, your first production will most likely be shot on MiniDV, which comes in the form of small, 60-minute tapes. The minimum price range for a quality camera in this case is around $1,500. When shooting on MiniDV, make sure to record in the SP (standard play) mode, not the LP (long play) mode, which greatly decreases the image and audio quality because not as much information is recorded on the tape.

There are also digital cameras that record directly to flash cards or hard disk drives instead of tape. However, keep in mind that the recording space is limited; approximately an hour in length. When the hard disk is filled, you must download the shot footage to a computer or external hard drive and erase the camera's hard drive to start recording new footage. This takes time and more equipment, such as a laptop computer on which to download your footage. Usually an extra person other than the camera operator is relegated to "media management" and making sure all the files get correctly downloaded to another computer. If you plan on shooting a live event that may be several hours in length, this type of camera would not be the best choice. However, there are cameras that are able to record to both tape and hard drive that eliminate the need for this extra step, saving both time and money.

Controls

The camera you choose should have manual controls over the basic functions, such as focus, exposure (iris), and audio levels. You do not want to be limited by the auto functions, although they can be a good guide initially when setting levels—for example, when setting the focus on a seated person you can turn the auto focus on to get them in focus, then turn it off. It is particularly handy to have the manual focus if you are doing artistic, rack-focus shots, such as showing a flower in focus, then focusing on the house behind in an establishing shot of a location. The more control you have over the image, the better.

There is also the question of screen formats and frame rates. Many cameras give you the choice of shooting in wide-screen (16:9) or television standard (4:3). Also, the frame rate can be changed. If something is shot at 30 frames per second, it will look like video. However, if it is shot at 24 frames per second, it will look like it has been shot on film.

> ## Objective
> > To choose a camera with the necessary functions that will make your documentary as good as it can be.

> ## Tip
> **Batteries**
> Take notice of how long the camera batteries last when they are fully charged. It is best to have at least two batteries and always make sure they are charged before you shoot. You can purchase a quick charger, which plugs into a normal wall outlet and can charge two batteries simultaneously.

Camera comrades
Current recording formats for cameras (from left to right) include SD memory cards, DVCAM, and MiniDV.

Prosumer vs. professional

A camera that is labeled as a "prosumer" simply means that it is intended for both the professional and the non-professional consumer. Such a camera will have auto settings for focus, aperture, zoom, and audio (for the consumer), while at the same time allowing manual controls for more precise settings. Prosumer cameras are also larger in size than a consumer camera.

Nowadays the gap between "home movie" cameras and professional television cameras is narrowing. Many current reality shows, documentaries, and television series utilize prosumer cameras, especially when there is a need for numerous cameras. Keep in mind that using a camera involves skill. Someone who knows how to shoot well with a $2,000 prosumer camera can obtain better images than a novice with a $60,000 camera.

Key features of the prosumer camera

> Manual control capability over focus, aperture, light, and audio.
> The majority of prosumer camcorders can handle low-light and have 3-chip color for better resolution.
> The button controls are positioned so that you can easily reach them while shooting —for example the zoom control, where your hand grips the side of the camera.
> Audio: These cameras have a built-in microphone and also input for an external microphone.
> Price: More expensive than consumer, less expensive than professional.

PROSUMER CAMERA:
LEFT SIDE AND RIGHT SIDE VIEWS

Handle grip

Additional controls for camera and side viewfinder

Built-in camera microphone

Viewfinder/ eyepiece

Pop-out monitor/ viewfinder

Built-in camera lens with lens shade

Videotape housing

Plug for external microphone

Record button

Manual focus ring

PROFESSIONAL CAMERA

Professional cameras feature removable lenses, larger imaging chips, better video and audio connections, and easily accessible manual controls. They are often shoulder mounted for steadier control and are larger than the prosumer camera.

● TECHNIQUE FILE

Check the low light

If you plan on shooting your documentary in a low-light scenario, make sure you have a camera that will perform well under those conditions. Some key points to consider:

*1 **Check the lens:** The wider the lens, the more light is needed.*
*2 **HD cameras need more light for a good image:** This defeats the purpose if you are shooting in a low-light scenario.*
*3 **Find someone locally:** Since you may not be able to test the camera beforehand, find someone who has the same camera.*
*4 **Read consumer reviews:** Find out as much as you can about specific cameras and ask other filmmakers for recommendations.*

The LCD screen (right)
Keep in mind that if your image looks good on the camera's pop-out LCD screen, it is good. In fact, it will most likely look better in editing, since the purpose of the screen is primarily for reference and has limited resolution.

Heed the zebras
A good way to check your lighting levels to make sure your shot is not too bright is to set your camera's "zebras" to 100. This is often a control setting on the side of the camera. When you turn this switch on, the viewfinder/screen will show visible lines on the brightest spots of the shot, like zebra stripes (as seen on the image, left). You simply have to iris down your shutter and make them go away to balance the brightness. There should still be a small number of these lines, however. It's always better to have the shot underexposed rather than overexposed, since you can correct that. (You cannot fix a shot that is overexposed.) Zebras are the best indication of your lighting levels.

> > > **Assignment 13**

List five or six things you need from the camera in order to shoot the documentary, such as:

> Must be able to shoot 24 frames per second
> Wide-screen option
> Wide-angle lens needed for some shots
> Needs to be able to record in low light
> Need to record on tape
> Long battery life

Defining your needs like this will make it easier for you to choose a camera that meets your specific requirements.

Using a tripod

If you are shooting the documentary and do not have a lot of experience, use a fluid-head tripod. You may have the best camera in the world, but if your camera moves are jerky and awkward it will convey to the viewer that your documentary is not of professional quality.

Below is a diagram indicating the ideal tripod setup for an interview.

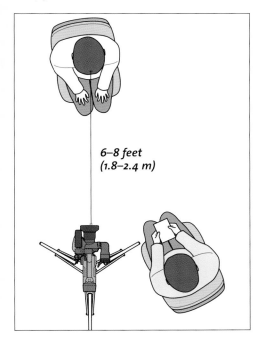

6–8 feet (1.8–2.4 m)

Positioning the tripod
The tripod/camera should be 6–8 feet (1.8–2.4 m) away from the interviewee, with the interviewer sitting either to the right or the left of the camera so that the subject looks at them, and not the camera. The tripod/camera should be at eye level, or slightly lower than the subject.

Lesson 12 : **Audio equipment**

The audio of a documentary is as important, if not more important, than your image. After all, someone will be willing to watch a program that looks "so-so" as long as they can hear it clearly. However, it is much more difficult for an audience to watch a crisp, clear picture with muffled or fluctuating sound. Bad audio will seriously compromise the quality of your production.

Microphones

The camera microphone is fine to use for ambient sound, such as when you are shooting footage in the country and want to hear the bird calls, but when interviewing you will need to use an external microphone that plugs into the camera. If you are shooting MiniDV with a prosumer camera, this will probably be a mini phono input. These are usually stereo, since there are two channels of audio available. This input is usually located near the built-in camera microphone. Once you plug the cable in here, it overrides the camera's microphone. However, you can purchase what is called an XLR adapter, a small box with two XLR inputs, that fits underneath or behind the camera. A mini phono plug connects this to the camera. XLR is the professional audio standard. This adaptor also gives you the option of recording the plug-in external microphone on one channel and the camera microphone on the other channel. This is good for backup or simultaneously recording ambient sound. Alternatively, you can hook up two external microphones to the adaptor, perhaps if you are interviewing two people at once.

There are two kinds of microphones you will need for shooting your documentary. The first is the lavalier or lapel microphone, which is small and clips onto a person's shirt or tie. It has to be well placed, and the person must remain stationary so that the microphone doesn't rub against their clothing and make a scratching noise. It can connect directly to the camera via a cable, or go through a wireless or radio microphone to avoid having to use a lengthy wire.

The second type of microphone is a directional or boom microphone that can be attached to a boom pole or set up on a microphone stand a few feet away from the person, out of camera range.

These microphones can cost from $100 to $1,000, depending on what you want to spend. Generally, the more expensive the microphone, the better it is, and your audio gear should cost one-quarter or more of the price of your camera.

Whichever type of microphone you use, make sure you record all of your interviews with the same type, otherwise the various pieces of footage will sound noticeably different.

> **Objective**

> Determine what type of microphone(s) will best suit your documentary based on where and how it will be shot. What will enable you to capture the best sound?

XLR connectors
These are used to connect high-quality professional microphones to equipment.

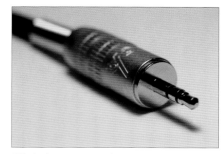

Mini phono connector
The majority of prosumer cameras will only have a mini phono jack to input an external microphone. The other end of the cable is probably an XLR connector that hooks to the microphone.

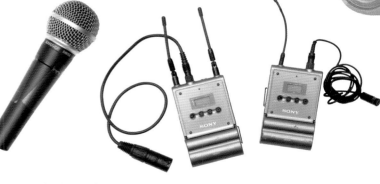

CAPTURING AUDIO

Different situations may require different types of microphones. On the right are some audio-capture patterns indicating the areas in which each type of microphone picks up sound in relation to its position, and the interview participants.

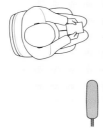

Shotgun mic
This is usually mounted on a boom and is used for picking up a single speaker's voice without much background noise. It has a very narrow recording area.

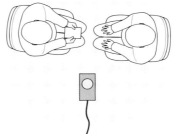

Multi-directional mic
This has a much wider recording area and is used to capture two or more people talking at the same time (such as a conversation). It is also used to record ambient sounds. The built-in camera microphones are multi-directional.

Lavalier mic
These are small microphones that are used for interviews and are clipped to the interviewee. They are also very directional and have a short pickup range, so not much background noise is picked up. They are often used in conjunction with a wireless transmitter (shown above), which eliminates the need for long audio cables.

Sound adjustment
An audio person directs a shotgun microphone to record a conversation between two of the interviewees. The microphone is covered in a "blimp" casing to prevent wind noise.

Headphones

It is a wise decision to invest in a good pair of headphones, because you need to listen to the audio while you are recording. If you hear that something is wrong, such as interference, you are unintentionally recording it. Remember, what you hear is what you are recording. If you are interviewing a person in his or her office and the air conditioning kicks on in the middle of the interview, be aware that you will not be able to get rid of that sound in the editing process. It is always best to correct the problem by doing another take while you are taping.

● **>>> Assignment 14**

Select three random sections of your documentary and list what type of microphone may be best suited for those sections, and why each type will work well in that situation.

For example:
• If interviewing a person in a crowded office, you will probably use a clip-on lavalier microphone, since it will pick up just the interviewee and not the background noise.

• If you are simply shooting B-roll of kids playing in a park and just need the ambient background noise, the built-in camera microphone will suffice.

• If you are interviewing someone who is walking around and talking, a directional microphone on a boom pole would work best, since the microphone will constantly need to be repositioned by a boom-pole operator.

Tip

Ensuring silence
When you are recording sound you must ensure that there is no background audio intrusion, such as ringing telephones or the hum of a refrigerator. You may want to put signs up, such as "Quiet Please—Recording Audio," if you are videotaping in an office that has many workers.

Get a good pair
If you are working on a very low budget you may be both the camera man and the audio person, but regardless, you should plan on spending between $40–$100 for a good pair of professional headphones. A good pair should be stereo, and will cover your entire ear, so that you only hear what is being recorded through the microphone. Since you will be wearing them for hours at a time, they must be adjustable and comfortable.

Bring your boom pole

For those shoots where there is lots of running around and little time for setting up, use an audio boom pole or "fish pole" to capture your audio. The directional microphone is attached to a shock mount on the end of the pole and a cable runs from the microphone, down the length of the pole, and to the camera audio input.

● *In inexperienced hands, the boom pole can cause problems; for instance, there may be a "rustling" or "knocking" noise from the cable or if the audio person is not holding the pole steady. It's worth getting new hands to practice before filming, or just use a microphone stand instead.*

● *For sit-down interviews a microphone stand will work fine. Point the microphone at the person's mouth, but make sure it and the stand are out of frame when you shoot.*

Take a stand
If you are doing a sit-down interview and a second person is not available to operate the boom pole, you can use a stationary microphone stand to hold the shotgun microphone in place.

Operation shotgun
It's important to point the shotgun microphone directly at the speaker's mouth. Imagine there is a straight line going from the tip of the microphone to the person's mouth and you'll get it right. Also, make sure the mic doesn't get into the camera frame—it's harder than it looks!

Lesson 13 : Lighting

Having a dependable light source is important when shooting, whether this means shooting outside in daylight or purchasing a lighting kit. The darker the image, the less resolution and more "grain" you will have in the picture. You want your camera to capture an image as well as it can so it can be as clear as possible.

Objective

> Ascertain what type of and how many lights you will need to illuminate your production, based on your various locations.

While you definitely need lights for interviews, you may not need them for additional footage you are shooting, such as the B-roll (see page 77).

The basics

The most basic lighting for your typical documentary/interview shoot will be two or three lights, which include stands, barn doors, and diffusion. These are for a key light (front), fill light (front side), and the backlight. The key light is the strongest light. The fill light is half the illumination of the key light, and the back light is 50–100 percent of the key light. So, if the key light is 500 watts, the fill will be 250 watts, and the backlight 250–500 watts.

Types of light

As with the camera and microphones, prices vary widely for lights. An average price, which includes the light and light stand, barn doors, and various types of diffusion, is around $150 to $200 per light. These are usually tungsten lights, though there are fluorescent and LCD video lights available. The bulbs for these lights cost $10–$30, and you must ensure that you have spare bulbs with you. These professional lights also get quite hot and need a cooling down period of 10–15 minutes before they are packed up. Your light case should be well padded to protect the lights and the fragile bulbs.

Lighting kits
Basic lighting kit packages are available for purchase at many video equipment retailers. They consist of three lights with barn doors and screens, cables, and stands, all of which fit snugly within the hard case.

Tip

Safety first
Safety is always important around lights, which are hot. But also consider the cables, making sure they are plugged in firmly and out of the way so that no one can trip over them. With this in mind, a light stand should never be placed over cables, since this makes it more prone to being knocked over, especially if one of those cables is moved.

Always wear gloves when you set up lights, and always have them facing away from you. They are extremely bright and hot.

There are also camera-mounted lights, which are usually powered with a separate battery. However, you must be within 8 feet (2.5 m) of your subject, and this light is rather harsh. It is useful if you are shooting something in a darkened room and placing lights on stands is not an option.

Since cameras are so good with low light nowadays, you can even get away with using hardware clamp lights, which use regular bulbs. The disadvantage of these is that you can't focus specifically the light as you would if you had barn doors.

Bear in mind that it is not wise to mix different sources of light, such as tungsten and fluorescent, because the color temperature is different when you white-balance the camera. Objects will appear either too red or too blue, depending on which light source they are closest to.

A good combination

In this sit-down interview, in which we see both the interviewer and interviewee, a combination of indoor and outdoor lighting is used to good effect.

LIGHTING SETUPS

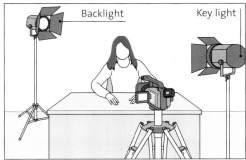

1 Lighting setup for two lights

The key light is set up off to the side of the camera, and a backlight is used to separate the interviewee from the background.

2 Lighting setup for three lights

The same as the set up for two lights, with the addition of a third fill light, in this case a light bouncing off of an umbrella reflector.

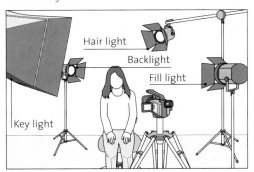

3 Lighting setup for four lights

In addition to the three-light set up, a fourth "hair light" is added to further separate the subject from the background.

LIGHTING FOR INDOOR INTERVIEWS

● *Lighting is most important for the people you are interviewing, especially if you are videotaping them indoors. Existing light is often not adequate and you will require a two- or three-light setup. Your main light will be 250–500 watts, a backlight should be half of that, and another light can be used as fill or to light up the background if needed.*

● *Of course, with more lights you can be more creative. Keep in mind that you should not cast shadows on the person's face, and make sure you can see the light reflected in their eyes; this makes them seem more alive and animated.*

● *Beware of light reflections if the interviewee is wearing glasses. For more on interview setups, see pages 92–93.*

WHAT TO WATCH

Hands on a Hard Body (1997)
This documentary depicts two dozen contestants competing in an endurance contest to win a brand new Nissan Hardbody truck. Shot outside, this film, unlike many others, uses natural lighting instead of artificial lighting.

Indoor lighting
Opposite is a four-light setup shown in context. Each of the four lights has its own purpose, but all work together to create the desired overall lighting effect. The fourth light (the key light) is out of the frame.

Tip

Don't forget the clothespins
Wooden clothespins are small but invaluable items that can be very handy when fastening pieces of diffusion to the front of a light. Fifty of these cost just a few dollars, and you only need two per light. They fasten the gel or diffusion to the barn doors and can withstand a great deal of heat, though you still want them as far away from the light as possible. Be careful not to buy wooden-looking clothespins that are actually made out of plastic, since these will melt and catch fire.

Setting up a backlight
For this particular interview, a backlight is set up to light the kitchen behind the interviewee.

Notice that an amber gel is placed on the light, to give it a warmer color, which fits nicely with the wood in the room.

The backlight illuminates the file cabinet behind the interviewee. For effect, a blue gel is used on the light.

The fill light helps to even out the key light and minimizes shadows on the face.

A second backlight illuminates the back of the interviewee, this time with an orange gel on it, for a warmer effect.

Stylized lighting

You may want the interviews in your documentary to have more precise lighting to make them stand out. For instance, you might want light casting shapes on the background through the use of "cookies," which are mounted on the front of the light to cast patterns, or you might want to use different colored gels. The more lights used, the longer the setup. Circumstances may dictate that you can use only one light, a camera-mounted light, if you are videotaping someone in a coal mine, for example.

Here a reflector is used for the main key light and a fill light is set on the opposite side of the camera.

There are two backlights: one, with an orange gel, casts warm light on the interviewee, and the other, with a blue gel, illuminates the background of the office.

Reflectors

When you are shooting a subject outside, make sure you have some reflectors, which can redirect the existing sunlight toward whatever it is you are shooting at. You'll usually need an additional person to do this, or you could clamp the reflector onto a light stand, though this can be difficult if it is windy outside. Reflectors can simply be a large white piece of card or a purchased reflector, such as a Flexfil.

● >>> Assignment 15

Pick three indoor interviews that are in different locations. On average, how many lights will you need to light them adequately?

Reflecting daylight
In this outdoor shoot, a reflector is redirecting daylight as the main source of light (therefore acting as a "key light") onto the interviewee.

Reflecting at night
A huge square reflector redirects light from three lights to create one large, soft-light source during this outdoor night shoot.

Lesson 14 : Editing equipment

Having shot your footage on digital video, you will need to edit digitally via a computer software program.

Objective

> To find an editing system that is capable of transforming your footage into the program that you have blueprinted and/or storyboarded. It is better to have a system that exceeds your needs.

KEY POINTS: Tools for editing

> Computer with enough RAM.
> External hard drive.
> Editing software.
> FireWire inputs.

To edit digital video, you need a non-linear editing program. Non-linear simply means you can easily, randomly access any of the video footage and arrange it in any manner without losing quality. Changing shots around, making a dissolve, a wipe, or completely recutting a scene is easily done with a few clicks of the mouse. You can think of it as word processing, only with images and sounds instead of words. All of your edits are kept track of in an edit decision list (EDL) in the program so your original footage remains unchanged.

The equipment

Your biggest piece of editing equipment is your Mac or PC. Decide what capabilities you need to complete your project, then shop around.

To do the actual editing, you will need editing software. Some basic video editing programs are included when you purchase a computer, but these are primarily intended for compiling home movies. You will most likely need something more versatile, with multiple video and audio tracks. Edit systems typically have 99 of each available. But before you purchase anything, determine what your budget is and make a list of what you need the editing system to do.

Costly, top-of-the-line edit systems have a computer system devoted solely to editing. With some edit systems, this hardware is made specifically to run the software. If you plan on using your computer, make sure that you have enough RAM to run the program and enough memory to store all of your video footage. This is particularly important with HD footage, which will take up twice the amount of space of standard digital footage. An external hard drive, usually a terabyte, is a good option. With editing, the more storage capability you have, the better, because video takes up a lot of megabytes per minute.

Three screens are better than one
Here, an editor works on a professional Avid editing suite. Note that he is using three monitors. The first shows his clip information, the middle shows both his footage and his edit along with the program's timeline, and the third shows the edited program.

Editing systems: The hardware

You'll need a dedicated system for editing and nothing else. Otherwise, you will get a bunch of glitches and problems which can cause your computer to crash, and mean you lose your time-consuming editing work. Remember, the more computer power you have the better, especially with high definition (HD). Aim for the fastest motherboard and processing power you can get, for example, a dual core Duo or Quad system on a Windows XP Platform, with 4 GB of RAM. Your editing capabilities will depend on how advanced or sophisticated your system is. Below is the basic system setup.

Primary monitor, which shows editing timeline and information.

Additional monitor to view edited footage.

External mixer, which is used to monitor the output sound. This just controls what you are listening to through the speakers and the headphones, since the actual sound editing is done via software.

External speaker.

Minimum requirements for your editing system

> Able to capture your footage format.
> Editing tools: transitions and titles.
> DVD creation, export for Web streaming.
> Output broadcast quality to digital tape format.

Editing systems: The software

The three leading non-linear video editing software programs are:

Final Cut Pro 7 (Apple, Inc.)
Premiere Pro CS5 (Adobe)
Avid Liquid Pro 7 (Pinnacle)

All three systems cost around $1,000. They are all professional, can edit both SD and HD video formats, and mixed formats, and have special effects and graphics capabilities, as well as output for streaming, DVD, and broadcast. These systems are very similar, but each offers its own niche or specialty, and each has its own loyal following. Choosing a system is a matter of personal taste, akin to the PC vs. Mac debate. We've outlined the key features below, to help you decide on what's best for you.

Operating systems

On a PC most editors use Windows XP, which is considered the most stable operating system from Microsoft. (Most editors do not work on Vista and/or Windows 7.) For Mac, Final Cut Pro (FCP) works on MAC OS X version 10.5.6 and higher.

Minimum storage

For storage memory (on your hard drive(s)), you should have at least 1 TB (terabyte) of hard-drive space for your editing. Audio/video files are huge, so you must have the space to allow your computer to handle and process these files effectively.

Transferring your footage

If you have shot onto tape, in order to get your footage to your editing system you need a video deck on which to play back the tapes. If all your footage has been stored on a video card or hard drive, it's just a matter of moving the files into your editing system. Purchasing a separate deck may cost more than what you paid for the camera; however, fortunately you can play the tapes back through the VTR function of your camera. You will also need to purchase a FireWire

Editing system	Mac/PC	Operating system	The review
Apple Final Cut Pro	Mac only	Mac OS X version 10.5.6 or later	> Considered the "professional editor's" choice. > Simplest to work and has the quickest learning curve. > Option to purchase Final Cut Express for a few hundred dollars; however, this program is missing some features, like "Cinema Tools." (But this is probably not needed for making a documentary.) >You can transfer your footage between Final Cut Express and Final Cut Pro if you upgrade to that program.
Adobe Premiere Pro CS5	Mac and PC	Mac OS 10.5.6 or later, Windows Vista, XP	> Advantage of seamless integration with other Adobe software, such as After Effects, Encore, and Photoshop. > More complicated than the others, so not easy to use. > Hardware has to be in pristine condition and dedicated to editing only.
Pinnacle Avid Liquid Pro 7	Mac and PC	Microsoft Windows XP SP2	> Integrated hardware and software platform, allowing for good performance and durability.

cable of 3–6 feet (1–1.8 m) to connect your camera to the computer. Through this cable you transfer all of your video/audio information.

Your editing system and computer also needs to be able to burn DVDs, since this is how you will be sending out review copies when you are finished. Another important requirement is that it also has a FireWire port, through which you will import all your footage from a video deck. Make sure that whichever you use will maintain the quality of your shot footage.

Other sources

In case you do not have an editing system or the means to purchase one, film students, or even people who work at the local television stations, may be willing to help. Make sure they are using a non-linear system and that they can devote the time you need to finish the project. However, if

you do this, make sure it is clear that they are following your instructions or that you are editing with them. This is your project and you are ultimately deciding how it is put together. That is not to say you can't be open to their suggestions; they may have good ideas and think of something that will only make the documentary better, particularly if they have a lot of editing experience. It is important to find a "like mind"; someone who agrees with your vision. The last thing you need is to be butting heads and disagreeing over content; it is a waste of everyone's time and you will only get frustrated. This is why it is wise to keep a copy of your edit and footage on an external hard drive so you can take it to another similar edit system. Always have a contingency plan.

It is entirely possible to learn the editing program on your own if you have the patience and time. After working on your own program for months, you will indeed become very familiar with its functions, which will make editing your next project a lot easier.

Tip
Transferring footage from MiniDV
Play MiniDV tapes only once or twice. They are fragile and the tape can crinkle after several plays. Rather than stopping and starting to input specific clips, it is safer and more time-efficient to simply capture the entire tape, then discard what you don't need at that point. It's not worth taking the chance that you will damage your tape.

Final Cut
Below is a screengrab from Final Cut software. From the labeling of shots and assembly of clips during your rough edit to color correcting and adding transitions and sound effects, there is a wealth of magical things such software can do.

> > > **Assignment 16**

Based on elements from your blueprint, list the five top functions you need your editing system (hardware and software) to accomplish, such as handling different tape formats/digital material, specific special effects, transitions, and video storage space. Remember, if you shot in HD you need an editing system that can work with HD.

SECTION 3

PRE-PRODUCTION

Pre-production is about putting together the "attack plan" for shooting your documentary. While your blueprint is a guide to how you wish your completed documentary to look, pre-production involves scheduling and more scheduling, lining up a crew if you have one, coordinating the individuals you are interviewing, setting up locations and getting permission to film at those locations, and even estimating how much tape stock you will need. Keep a notebook, keep a calendar, and plan to shoot everything within a few months.

Getting organized

Pre-production involves a lot of mixing and matching of people, places, and resources, but because you're the producer, it's all up to you. The more thorough your pre-production is, the more smoothly your actual production will go. Think of it as a preemptive aspirin to prevent a production headache.

Schedules

The shooting schedule represents your timeline, from days to weeks to months, so try to be as detailed as possible. In many instances other people's schedules will determine your shooting schedule. Tell your interviewees when you would like to start shooting and find out the days and times they are available. They are usually helpful and will give you a few options. After all, they did agree to be in your documentary.

Be realistic about your schedule. It is probably not wise to interview ten people in one day. The rule of thumb is that everything will always take longer than you think. One day you may only have one interview scheduled, which will take two hours, but you must figure in the hour to drive there, maybe

an hour to set up at the location, a half-hour to pack up all of the equipment, and then the hour back: a total of five and a half hours.

Crew

Organizing crew members may pose more difficulty. To find them, go to the video department of your local community college and put up a flyer, and place advertisements on the Internet. Be upfront as to whether or not any pay is involved. Make your project sound enticing and ensure that your crew is enthusiastic. As the producer, the person in charge, you must have an answer to all of their questions, which is where your blueprint comes in handy.

Once you have picked your crew, ask them to give you a schedule of when they are available. Keep in mind that it may get more complicated when the person you are having operate the camera is also the owner of that camera and they are only available on specific days. It is good practice to have a contingency plan for last-minute changes, such as them getting a flat tire on the way to a location or having to scrap the day's entire shoot because of a tornado sighting.

CONTENTS — PAGES

Lesson 15 :
Self-funding vs. investors

Whether you decide to self-fund or pursue investors, it is recommended that you formally establish a business to produce the documentary. This specific business very much depends on what your documentary is about and the type of investors you wish to pursue.

Sole proprietor

The easiest business to establish is the sole proprietorship, which is simple to set up and does not cost very much. It can most often be done through your local city government. There is no distinction between the sole proprietorship and yourself, so your taxes can be done on the same form. Plus, you can deduct your business expenses on your yearly taxes, which is a plus when you are producing the documentary. The downside is that if your company is sued, perhaps as a result of some type of accident, the lawyers can go after your personal belongings and assets.

Corporation

Setting up a corporation involves much more work, including keeping detailed paperwork and records as well as paying yearly fees and taxes. Because a corporation is considered a separate legal entity, it is taxed separately and has its own assets and liabilities. If for some reason there are lawsuits against the company, your individual assets are protected.

There are two types of corporation: the for-profit and the non-profit. A for-profit corporation shares its profits with the owners, shareholders, and investors. If you make millions of dollars from your project, the money is split among everyone.

The profit made by a non-profit organization is reinvested back into the company, to pay for items such as equipment and office supplies.

However, in a non-profit you can pay yourself a certain salary, so you are able to make money. The stipulation to establish a non-profit, however, is that its mission is to benefit the "public good," through charitable, educational, religious, or scientific means. If your documentary will somehow benefit society, it may be possible to establish a non-profit company to produce it. However, if you established the business just to make a single documentary, then you'd have to eventually close down the business when it was completed. If you plan on making more documentaries under the company name, this is not a problem.

> **Objective**
> > Decide how much time and energy you want to spend on funding options. What is the most realistic way for you to get your project off the ground?

KEY POINTS: Limited liability

> The best option as a first-time documentary maker may be to form a limited liability company.
> The paperwork is that of a sole proprietorship, and the income is included as part of your individual tax form.
> Your personal assets are protected if you go into debt or are sued.
> As with all the other aspects of production, the more prepared and preemptive you are, the better.

Sourcing investment

There is no harm in trying to get investors for your project, even if you do think you can get by without them. You want to make the best program you can, so if you can get money to produce your documentary, fantastic. The worst scenario is that they say no. If you have an investor you will most likely have a bigger budget, which allows for more travel, better equipment, and more crew, if needed. Potential investors could be anyone from local businesses to a wealthy relative. Be prepared for any questions they have and also be clear and thorough about it. Written materials, such as a description of the documentary and where you plan to market it, are helpful to them. You want them to visualize your program, so show them your material, perhaps in a portfolio. Include your proposed budget, which depends on the scope of the project. Is there much travel involved? Do you need to purchase a new computer and editing equipment? Do you need to pay yourself to work on the documentary? Do you need to pay the crew? All of this is acceptable and should be listed in your detailed budget.

It is important that you are comfortable with the agreement you make with your investors. In a typical agreement, all the investors get a total of 50 percent of the profits, so if you have two equal investors they would each get 25 percent of the profits. While you do intend to make all your money back and hopefully a profit, guarantee

Avoid product placements

Do not take money from a company if it's in return for placing their product somewhere in the program. An example of this is featuring numerous shots of a piece of exercise equipment in a physical fitness documentary. Not only will it make your documentary seem like an infomercial, but it will also be unacceptable for such venues as PBS. Product placement can compromise the documentary for obvious reasons.

them nothing. After all, this is a risky business and making a fortune is not guaranteed. Other investors may simply give you money in the form of a contribution, because they like the project and support it.

Keep in mind that some companies will only give money to non-profits, and then again only to certain non-profits they have supported for years. However, there is a way to possibly get this money without having to form a non-profit corporation yourself, by finding what is called a fiscal sponsor. Let's say that you are doing a documentary on people suffering with a specific form of cancer. You then approach a cancer-related, non-profit group to be a sponsor. If you have a similar purpose and goals, they may be interested. Under this arrangement, your documentary becomes a project of this particular non-profit, so you can use their status to solicit these specific investors. They will also manage all of the incoming and outgoing funds for the documentary. In return, they'll get a small percentage of the monies received to make it worth their while.

Portfolio

You may not be talking to your investors face-to-face and as a result, you may be e-mailing them your portfolio and information rather than giving them a hard copy; however, it should include:

> A synopsis of the documentary (see page 23).
> The intended audience.
> The various locations where it will be filmed.
> The people/experts you will interview (the "cast").
> The venue in which it will be shown/available (PBS, local TV, festivals, DVD).
> The documentary's budget (see page 62).
> Previous credits/demo reel of the director/producer.
> Contact information for the director/producer.

● TECHNIQUE FILE

Writing a budget

When writing the budget for your documentary, list the actual costs for services and be as specific as possible to ensure that prospective investors get the right impression. Investors expect that you'll be paying yourself and/or other people. On the right is an example breakdown of costs to help you.

Break down the costs into production and post-production.

Production costs (20 days)

Producer/director/shooter ($350.00 per day at 20 days) $7,000.00	
Production assistant ($150 per day at 20 days)	$3,000.00
Transportation (gas and flights)	$2,000.00
Expendables (misc.)	$500.00
Video tape stock	$500.00
Camera and audio	$3,000.00
Editing/Final Cut Pro/hard drive	$3,000.00

Instead of writing down three months for production time, write down the specific number of days you plan to spend shooting and editing.

Post-production costs (30 days)

Editor ($250 per day)	$7,500.00
Original music	$1,000.00
Closed-captioning	$1,500.00
Betacam/digital mastering costs	$500.00

Once program is completed

Phone/mail/shipping	$1,000.00
DVD duplication (reviews/press/screeners)	$500.00
DVD box artwork	$500.00

Total budget:

$24,500.00

The true budget
Although a specific number of days is listed in this budget, this really only reflects the minimum. Many more hours and days will go into the shooting and editing of the documentary than specified here.

If you already own the camera and editing equipment, you are ahead of the game, but it's better to have a larger budget to show investors. You're likely to obtain only a portion of "what's needed" to get the production started.

TECHNIQUE FILE

Sell special credits for cash

One way of generating income is to "sell credits" in the documentary, so that for a set price a company or person's name will be listed in the "Special Thanks" section of the end credits. You can also ask for contributions, which would be handled the same way. However, you will have to tiptoe around this in regard to your local PBS policy.

Self-funding

You may wait months, if not years, to acquire investors and grants, particularly if this is your documentary debut and you don't yet have a solid track record. If you don't want to deal with the work and time of finding them and wish to dive right into production, self-funding may be your best option. You do not need a fortune to make a documentary, but can create a broadcast-quality program for next to nothing.

If this is the route you are taking, it's best to start with a local topic within a reasonable driving distance. In fact, you may very well be limited in terms of access to production and editing equipment as well, which will involve creative scheduling. On the plus side, there will be less pressure because you don't have to "deliver the goods" at a specific time and can work at your own pace. You can always get sponsors and grants after the program is shot and edited, especially if it is intended for television, such as for PBS.

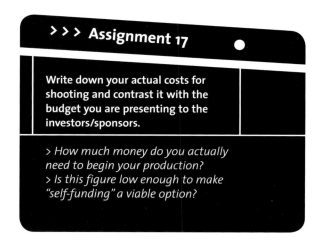

>>> **Assignment 17**

Write down your actual costs for shooting and contrast it with the budget you are presenting to the investors/sponsors.

> *How much money do you actually need to begin your production?*
> *Is this figure low enough to make "self-funding" a viable option?*

Lesson 16 : Obtaining underwriters for television

Obtaining funding through underwriters—financial sponsors—can be done at any time. It is much more likely to happen, though, if you are already in production or after the production is completed and the program is edited. Companies are more apt to agree to become sponsors when they can see the actual program. They are even more likely to say yes if the film has already been accepted to be broadcast on television.

Underwriters have no say as to how the program is put together, and cannot provide any sort of paid product placement if it's for a venue like PBS. If you made a documentary on diabetes that featured the National Diabetes Society, you could not have them as an underwriter, because it gives the perception of product placement and compromises the integrity of the documentary. Unlike an investor, an underwriter does not expect a return on their money. They are supporting the production and are basically paying for an advertisement and association with the program.

Abiding by the rules

The Public Broadcasting Service (PBS) has specific rules for underwriter credits. All entities providing funds to a program must be acknowledged, either at the beginning or end of the program. They can't be identified in the production credits, such as in the "Special Thanks" section. If they are being acknowledged at the beginning, they are each allowed a maximum 15-second slate, which includes the sponsor's logo, information, and even a voice-over. The total time allowed for sponsors at the beginning is one minute, so if you have six sponsors, they would get 10 seconds each. If you have only two sponsors, then it would be 30 seconds each. This underwriter acknowledgment block is referred to as the "underwriting pod."

> ## Objective
> > Determine the most likely sponsors/ underwriters for your program. Who will see this as an opportunity to benefit from an association with the documentary?

● >>> Assignment 18

Draft your own proposal for selling your documentary to potential sponsors.

You should include:
1) Your company information
2) How this will be of benefit to your sponsors/underwriters
3) What your sponsors get out of it (publicity, etc.)

PBS rules

The PBS website lists the following rules for underwriters.

> Must be acknowledged at the beginning or end of the program.
> No underwriter should exceed 20 words past "This program is made possible by X."
> An underwriter credit may not contain qualitative claims, calls to action, comparisons, pricing information, or any other language that is deemed promotional.
> A product manufactured by an underwriter may be mentioned once at the head of the underwriter, immediately following identification. (Example: SprocketCo, maker of Sprockets.) The brand name may not be repeated.
> No more than five products or services may be mentioned or listed.
> An underwriter credit may not feature a sung jingle. Music is allowable; music with words is not.
> Slogans that contain calls for action, qualitative claims, pricing information, or other objectionable language are not allowable even if they are established.
> Product placement, or the perception of product placement, must be avoided.

Drafting a proposal

In order to "sell" your documentary to an underwriter/sponsor, you'll need to put together a proposal that effectively summarizes key points of interest. Here is a sample proposal. Use this as a template from which to build your own.

Proposal for *"I'm Not Nuts": Living With Food Allergies*

Company information
Brimstone Media Productions, LLC, which was first established in NYC in 1992, is an independent video production company now located in Brighton, Michigan. Brighton is located approximately one hour from Detroit. To date, the company has produced six documentaries that have aired on PBS and other cable stations.

Grant providers and corporate sponsors
Grant and corporate sponsors will receive prominent acknowledgment of their funding contributions at the very beginning of the broadcast documentary. It will be the first thing viewers see and hear, as the written acknowledgment will also be accompanied by a voice-over. Institution/company logos and contact information will give contributors exposure, similar to an advertisement. Specific mention of products and/or services can be included in this sponsorship information as well. PBS acknowledges all of their major grant makers and corporate sponsors in this way. This sponsorship will also be included in the DVD copies that are sold.

Distribution outlets
After the project is completed, the filmmakers intend to distribute the documentary locally and nationally to such broadcast entities as Michigan Public Television and the National Public Television System. NETA, a company that supplies programming nationally to PBS, has already voiced interest in this program upon its completion.

There are 360 PBS stations across the United States. (A few stations in Canada receive these PBS broadcasts as well.) It is estimated that 70 per cent of these stations have broadcast the filmmaker's previous health-related documentary. As a result, inquiries were received throughout the past four years from many people and institutions positively acknowledging the program and requesting ordering information.

In addition, as mentioned above, there are excellent and important opportunities for distribution through the educational market, hospitals, universities, and public libraries. The home video market is an arena unto itself and is reached through PBS broadcasts and websites.

The filmmaker has strong personal contacts in all of these distribution areas, as well as in others, as his successful distribution history attests to. (Please see "About the filmmaker" below.) In turn, sponsors have an excellent chance of receiving a wide range of media exposure and name recognition, both at the local and national levels.

Specifics about PBS sponsorship
There are 360 PBS stations in the United States. It is estimated that 25 to 60 per cent of the total number of PBS stations across the country (and some additional ones in Canada) will broadcast the *"I'm Not Nuts": Living With Food Allergies* program. The stations will have the right to broadcast the program for an unlimited number of times, for a period of five years. It is up to the individual stations to determine the time and date of all broadcasts.

The documentary is allowed to secure four sponsors (15 seconds each, 1 minute total). In this fifteen seconds, the sponsor's logo, still image, or video clip can appear and their website and phone number can be displayed for five seconds, according to set PBS sponsorship rules. Specific mention of health-related products and/or services can also be included in this sponsorship information.

Sponsorship amount
In regards to a recommended sponsorship fee, the filmmakers propose a one-time contribution of $_____ . Please remember that this amount is for a five-year period of time for the PBS/television broadcasts.

The above stated amount is a recommendation based on how much the program cost to produce and the audience exposure sponsors are anticipated to receive. This proposed fee is negotiable. The producer is more than willing to discuss specific contribution amounts with potential sponsors.

Additionally, sponsors will receive a number of free VHS/DVD copies of the completed program as part of their sponsorship. Specific needs should be discussed directly. For any questions or comments please contact:

Kevin J. Lindenmuth Brimstone Media Productions, LLC
Phone/Cell/E-mail:

Your proposal should include information on:

1 Your company: Provide an introduction to your company; you may want to mention previous documentaries if you think this will give you more clout.

2 Benefits to the sponsor: Outline the advantages—how will contributors be credited/acknowledged? Mention specific exposure to logos, products, or services.

3 Distribution: Provide a summary of the distribution outlets through which the documentary will be channeled. The idea is to really "sell" this to the sponsor, and make it look like an attractive proposal: the more exposure, the better.

4 PBS specifics: Include any specific information about PBS —detail broadcasting stations, timings, and exposure permitted by the service.

5 The amount: Your proposal should include your proposed (hoped-for) fee, and brief a account of what this fee will cover.

6 Contact details: Don't forget to insert your name, e-mail address, and telephone number(s); should sponsors be interested in contributing or have further questions, this information should be easily accessible.

Lesson 17 : **Scheduling shoot days**

Scheduling involves bringing together not only the elements of your availability, but that of the equipment, crew, interviewees, and locations, and whether the order you shoot in has a bearing. Your schedule establishes a timeline for completing the entire shoot.

Shooting without a schedule
Below is an example of a documentary for which little could be scheduled. Produced and directed by Jessica Vale and Nika Offenbac, Small, Small Thing *examines violence against women and children in post-conflict Liberia. The documentary includes interviews with victims, their families, the accused, non-government organizations, everyday Liberians, and community groups to create an accurate portrait of the community, and the governmental response to these crimes. Because of the location, various people involved, and delicate situation, the majority of the shoot could not be planned before the filmmakers' arrival in the country. Capturing the footage they needed would turn out to be somewhat of an adventure and really drew upon the filmmakers' ability to improvise.*

Of course, it isn't always possible to establish a timeline. As a documentary maker, you are entirely at the mercy of your subject matter and will often have to shoot as and when you can, i.e., when participants are available. Unless your documentary is strictly scripted and you know all of the specific shots you need, it is difficult to plan a schedule months in advance. There are, however, some key considerations that will impact your order of work and more crucially, your timing; it's important to be aware of these when scheduling your shoot days.

1 The first interviews were conducted inside the Liberian Parliament building. The crew and interviewees had to move locations because it started raining during the first interview. They had to tip the security to get into the nearest building they could.

2 These interviews were conducted on the same day as the previous interview (1), a few blocks away in a slum between neighborhoods. When working in foreign countries, it's really helpful if you can work with local people and producers who know their way around the places you want to get to. This was the second of four shoots we did on that day.

3 This shot and the next (4) were taken a few days later in the abandoned cemetery in the center of Monrovia.

Time and place

Once you have secured your equipment and have a clear idea of when you want to begin shooting, it is time to schedule the specific shoot days. If you have a script, this means breaking down your scenes, bearing in mind whether you need to shoot in a particular order. For example, you may need to interview a man before and after his gastric bypass surgery, and possibly six months later to visibly show his rapid weight loss. These considerations will have an impact on your scheduling.

Locations may also have a determining factor. Let's say you are doing a documentary on a local haunted house, which is going to be demolished in two months. This does not leave you much time. You need to get both exterior and interior coverage for your editing now, because there is no going back after the demolition. It becomes more complicated if you need to interview a well-known psychic talking about the house in the house, and he is only available the one day you planned to shoot something else. Then the scheduling becomes a matter of prioritizing which interviews and shots you need the most. You may find yourself bending over backward to get the specific shot or interview you need.

Scheduling interviews

There are two ways to go about scheduling interview shoots. One is to let the interviewees know the days you want to shoot and have them pick a day and a backup day in case of last-minute occurrences. The other option is to find out when they are available for shooting, and schedule according to that information. You will often find yourself doing both. Remember, the people you are interviewing have lives and jobs. You may have to shoot around holidays, birthday parties, and sickness.

KEY POINTS: Scheduling factors

> Your availability.
> Equipment availability.
> People availability.
> Location availability.
> Does it matter what order. you shoot the interviews?

>>> Assignment 19

List three locations you are interested in using in your documentary.

> Do you anticipate any difficulty shooting at these places?
> What will you have to do to secure the location? (See page 69.)

4 *Scheduling this location was really based on the availabilty of the girl pictured, and her stories. After the war, she lived in the hollowed-out tombs in the cemetery.*

5 *Working with non-government organizations can be tricky. This shoot took place in a safe house for child victims. It was rescheduled three times as a result of various interruptions.*

6 *You can never rely on travel options in rainy season. This shot was taken about halfway through a nine-hour drive on dirt roads. Always expect the worst, and make provisions for the fact that you might not be able to get where you need to go!*

Lesson 18 : **Release forms**

The purpose of the release form is to prevent any sort of misunderstanding over your production, giving you legal permission to film a person.

No matter whom you videotape, they must sign a release form. This form states that they are giving you permission to use their image in the documentary. This protects you from any future claims. If someone refuses to sign the release form, you must not videotape them. For example, they may say they will only sign a release form after they see the edited documentary. Perhaps they don't like how they look—a reaction that happens far more often than you would expect. They could then decide not to be in it, at which point you have to edit them out and therefore change the complete flow of the documentary. This wastes both your time and theirs.

Although you will probably never need to refer to these documents once they are signed, it is important to file them away in a safe place in case they are required in the future—sometimes distributors want to see copies of them.

Personal/photo release

Anyone interviewed on camera or shown in close-up needs to sign a photo release form. Make sure you have plenty of these forms printed; it is a huge nuisance trying to track people down and get them to sign it afterward. Mail them a copy ahead of time.

Unlike professional actors, interviewees rarely receive compensation other than to receive a credit and a copy of the final product. This, too, is written into the release form, which features their signature, address, and phone number.

If you are videotaping a contained group of people, such as some type of support group or a meeting, you can modify this release form into a "blanket release" and have them all sign their name on the same sheet of paper.

PHOTO RELEASE/ADULT

For valuable consideration received, I hereby grant to (your name/ company)_____the absolute and irrevocable right and unrestricted permission in respect of video or still imagery or in which I may be included with others, to use, publish, and republish the same in whole or in part, individually or in any and all media now or hereafter known, and for any purpose whatsoever, for illustration, promotion, art, editorial, advertising, and trade, or any other purpose whatsoever without restriction, I hereby release and discharge (your name/company)_____from any and all claims and demands arising out of or in connection with the use of the images, including without limitation any and all claims for libel or violation of any right of publicity or privacy.

This authorization and release shall also insure to the benefit of the heirs, legal representatives, licensees, and assigns of _____ as well as the person(s) of whom were photographed.

I am of full age and have the right to contract in my own name. I have read the foregoing and fully understand the contents thereof.

This release shall be binding upon me and my heirs, legal representatives, and assigns.

Date_____

Business or Community Name_____

Name_____

Signature_____

Address_____

Phone_____

This generic release form for an adult can be modified. The release for a minor requires a parent's or guardian's signature. This is not legal advice and for such you should consult an entertainment lawyer.

Location release

Location release forms are used for private residences and grant you permission to shoot on the property for a specified time period, and to bring crew and equipment. The release will stipulate that you are responsible for any damages caused during the production of the documentary.

Get this release form signed days ahead of your actual shoot because it locks in that particular location. Once the property owner has signed it, they can't change their mind or tell you to shoot on a different day.

Leave as you find
When shooting on a private property, you'll need to move things around to make space for the crew and set up lighting. Be sure to restore all at the end of the shoot—there should be no signs of you ever being there!

LOCATION RELEASE

Permission is hereby granted to _____ ("Producer") and its employees, agents, independent contractors, and suppliers to enter in the property located at_____ _____ (the "Property") for the purpose of photographing and recording certain scenes for a commercial. For the amount of $_____ the sufficiency of which you acknowledge, you agree to the statements and conditions stated in this contract concerning your Property.

Use of Property
Producer may use the inside and outside of the Property located at
_____
from the day of _____ to the day of _____ during the hours of _____ to _____. Producer will use the Property as a location for photographing, videotaping, and/or making sound recordings. In the event of a delay in schedule due to photographically unfavorable conditions, or reasons beyond our control, Producer holds the right to reschedule at the agreed fees and terms provided in this agreement. Producer may photograph, film, videotape, and record sound on the Property and use the resulting materials in any way Producer chooses.

You give us permanent, worldwide, exclusive right to own all rights to all Producer records and photographs. You agree to have no right to inspect or approve recordings.

Producer may bring into the Property our crews, actors, and equipment. Producer may construct temporary sets and, after completing photography and recording, will restore the Property to its original condition as of the initial date of occupancy by _____ unless otherwise agreed to by both parties in writing, reasonable wear and tear excepted. You give us the right to assign all terms stated in this contract. You agree to waive any further compensation or demand of any kind forever.

Producer agrees to hold you harmless from any liability and loss which may be caused by our employees or equipment.

You understand the terms described in this contract. You are over 18 years of age. You have the authority to sign this contract and grant us the rights given under this contract.

Date _____ Signature _____
Print name_____
Address _____
_____
Phone _____
S.S. # _____

This generic release form can be modified.
This is not legal advice and for such you should consult an entertainment lawyer.

Lesson 19 : Insurance vs. no insurance

Your decision as to whether to get insurance for your production depends on your peace of mind and your budget. Several different kinds of insurance are available for a documentary in production, including production insurance, production equipment insurance, and insurance for errors and omissions. Regardless of whether you do or do not purchase insurance, the key is always to take care when you are in production.

Walking on the wild side
Wildlife photographers (2) know how unpredictable—and potentially dangerous—their subjects can be. Insurance is a must!

> Objective

> To decide whether having insurance is a necessity or not. Will it make your production run smoothly and make you more comfortable?

KEY POINTS: To insure or not to insure?

> Is your shoot potentially hazardous?
> Is there a chance your equipment will get damaged?
> Is any of the footage you are using copyrighted? If so, do you have the signed clearances to use that footage?

Production insurance

Production insurance protects producers against general liability, automobile liability, and safety of the cast and crew. It is expensive and covers only a month or two of shooting. Assuming your production does not involve stunts, deep-sea dives, pyrotechnics, or transporting equipment by mule up the side of a thousand-foot cliff, a lack of insurance probably isn't an issue. However, if you are worried that something could happen during the production, you should contact several insurers to see what your options are. In fact, some of the locations you want to shoot at may require that you have insurance.

Production equipment insurance

Production equipment insurance is usually purchased if you own hundreds of thousands of dollars of equipment that you want protected against theft and damage. The more affordable prosumer digital cameras often have additional insurance that can be bought at the store it was purchased from. If you are renting equipment from a rental house, insurance coverage is part of the rental price.

Watch your step
Filmmakers shooting in an abandoned factory (1)—a hazardous location—should be insured and so protected in the event of an accident at work. On the more precarious camera setups (3), it's often good to have a second person watching your back, as assurance.

Errors and omissions insurance

Errors and omissions (E & O) insurance indemnifies producers against lawsuits that may arise from the content of a production. This would include lawsuits alleging copyright infringement, invasion of privacy, plagiarism and infringement on title, slogan, or trademark, and libel or slander against a person or product. If you are making a confrontational documentary about how a noted chemical plant is dumping toxins into the nearby river, you probably need this type of insurance. You can bet Michael Moore does not shoot anything without it.

No insurance

A low-budget documentary may not be able to afford any insurance, the cost of which can come in at more than that of the actual production. This does not necessarily prevent you from making your program. See if there is a way to make your documentary under the banner of an established production company so you can make use of their insurance coverage. Establish a corporation or a limited liability company (LLC) so that your personal property is protected. You may even choose to modify your talent and location releases, stating that you are not responsible for any injury or accidents during a shoot.

> > > **Assignment 20**

Does your production involve many locations or just one? A lot of people or just a couple? Is expensive production equipment in precarious situations? Make a list of everything that needs to be considered and then use it to ascertain if your production is at high risk for any type of mishap. What are the odds?

Case study: *Planning a documentary*

When planning your documentary, it's crucial that you are passionate about the idea behind it, since your passion is what will encourage other people to get involved. In the following article (the first case study of three), Kevin Lindenmuth gives his own personal account of the planning process that preceded the shooting of his documentary, *The Life of Death*. See pages 94–97 to see how the filming developed, and pages 134–135 for the post-production process.

Choosing the subject: The idea behind the documentary

Having completed several health-related documentaries (multiple sclerosis, food allergies) and a spiritually themed program (*The Healing Prophet: Solanus Casey*, 2006), the subject for my next documentary became apparent: death. All of my work is personal and this was no different. As you get older and friends and relatives pass away, death comes to the forefront of your thoughts. Yet, how exactly should one go about tackling this as a subject for a documentary? First I needed to consider the target audience.

The audience

Since everyone thinks about their demise at one point or another, the topic of death has universal appeal, and so it will also have the widest potential audience. Death is often thought of as a taboo, perhaps even horrific topic, and so the subject tied into my experience as an independent director/producer/writer of several horror films. Thematically, it fit in with all aspects of my previous video production work.

Researching the subject

Research on the Internet revealed that while there are many documentaries about death—both the physical process

of death and the emotional impact of loss—there are not many about the concept or idea of dying. This was to become the crux of my documentary: different people's perceptions of death. It would be based around interviewees' personal experiences of loss and their understanding of how death is perceived by the general public.

An initial list of questions to elicit information from the interviewees was made. These questions were expanded upon after the interviewees were actually chosen.

The title

Since the concept of death often takes on a life of its own in film, news, and other media, the title came to me very quickly: *The Life of Death*. I did some checking on the Internet Movie Database, as well as numerous online search engines, and the title was certainly original. It accurately sums up what the program is about and piques people's interests, and crucially, it's short and memorable.

Funding/budget

My experience has taught me that it's much easier to obtain funding for a documentary that is aimed at a specific viewership, such as my earlier films about living with multiple sclerosis

which received some of their funding from pharmaceutical companies producing MS medications. However, while *The Life of Death* would have a potentially huge audience, it was too broad a concept for an investor or PBS underwriter. There's ultimately nothing being cured or sold.

The idea for the documentary had come quickly and the prospect of waiting six months to garner unlikely sponsors or investors was not appealing. It therefore became a self-funded production with budget considerations. Because of this, interviews were limited to Michigan and New York City. I live in Michigan and I was going to New York City for an unrelated editing gig where I could work on this project at the same time. The biggest costs would be tape stock and paying for taxis to take me to the various locations; the biggest hardship would be lack of sleep.

Choosing the interviewees

Since the documentary's objective was to convey the information and emotion through the people being interviewed, these individuals needed to be articulate, intelligent, and good on camera. They also had to be different enough from each other in personality; some serious, some funny. I considered all the people I knew or was acquainted with who would make good subjects and lived in either Michigan or New York City. For example, I worked with some of the actors from my NYC independent filmmaking days and was introduced to many of the writers and filmmakers when I had interviewed them for magazines or websites. Almost immediately I had a list of more than a dozen interesting candidates. This seemed to work out great, because one of the themes of the documentary would be how death is portrayed in the media, and they all worked in some aspect of it.

Pre-planning

Planning is everything. First, I wrote a short synopsis of the documentary that I could e-mail to the potential interviewees, and also included the list of interview questions. I sent all of this information to them several months before the start of the production.

Interviewees selected

Nearly all of the individuals I contacted were interested and enthusiastic about participating in the documentary. I managed to secure thirteen interviewees in total: a few from Michigan, a couple from Cleveland, Ohio, and the rest based in New York City.

Two quotes were included at the end of the synopsis to convey the "feel" of the project— one serious and one humorous.

Subject: The Life of Death
From: Kevin Lindenmuth
To: David Crumm

Feature-length documentary: *The Life of Death*

What it's about:
For almost everyone (alive that is) death is something that looms far off on the horizon, and although it is an unavoidable reality, the concept of it can differ widely from person to person.

This documentary will explore how death is perceived by a wide range of people who work in the media (writers/performers/singers/filmmakers), and how death influences how they go about their lives. The program is about the concept of death taking on a life of its own.

"Live as if you were to die tomorrow. Learn as if you were to live forever."
Mahatma Gandhi

"I wanna die peacefully in my sleep like my grandpa, not screaming like the other people in his car."
Will Shriner, comedian

It is important to meet with your talent prior to any videotaping, to make sure they photograph well. Sometimes, if they are a noted expert, you have to deal with what you're given.

Continues on next page

The style

There would be no narration and the documentary was unscripted, although the questions the interviewees were answering would help to structure the film. It is a first-person account of the interviewees' experiences.

Scheduling the interviews

The individuals living in the Metro-Detroit area were available for interviews much sooner than those in NYC, so their interviews were scheduled first. I was in New York for two weeks, so I scheduled all of the New Yorker interviews within this time period, with each interview requiring no more than a few hours.

As for the interview locations, I asked if I could interview them at their apartments or at their place of work. One interview proved more difficult to arrange: the interviewee was only available from 3–4 pm on weekdays, and could not be shot at his apartment or his workplace. I pulled in a few favors and eventually arranged to shoot him at a different studio where another friend of mine works.

I wrote everything down in my schedule book and told everyone I would confirm a few days before their individual interviews. The number one priority was videotaping all of these interviews. Location would not make or break this documentary, since the focus is the individuals and their thoughts.

Fine tuning
Once the interviewees are chosen, the original list of questions is refined, ready for shooting. Since these questions will form the backbone of the documentary, it's important to get these right.

Questions for The Life Of Death

1 Do you think that death is more powerful to the human mind than life? (For example, are you more likely to say "I want to do _____ before I die" rather than "I want to do _____ because I'm alive?")
2 Do you think a person's attitude toward death affects how they live their life?
3 How has death affected/influenced your profession?
4 What do you want to do before you die?
5 Death is an idea, only known through the death of others and people's opinions about it. What is your take on death?
6 What do you think happens to you after you die? What do you want to happen?
7 Has someone close to you died? Talk about this.
8 Do you think that people are more concerned with what they believe will happen to them after death than the actual, physical process of dying?
9 A lot of religions say that if you don't believe in a certain way of life, bad things will happen to you after you are dead. What is your opinion about this?
10 In your experience, what religions are more accepting of death?
11 In America, it seems like people view death as a failure. If someone has cancer or another disease they have to "fight it" (fight death), and if they lose, they have "lost their battle," and a sense that if they've died, they didn't work hard enough. Where do you think this attitude comes from?
12 Do you think that horror and death in books, movies, and on television appeals to the younger crowd because death is almost like a fantasy, in the sense that it's something that's impossible?
13 Do you think that the media in general makes people fear death so they'll buy things (such as "buy this because it may prolong your life," or "Watch tonight how you can live longer..." etc)?
14 Do you think people are out of touch with death or the idea of death because they are out of touch with nature? People don't encounter death firsthand anymore, except when they go to a funeral, which makes it more of an alien concept.
15 How do you think your concept of death has changed over the years? Is there a particular experience of someone dying that has affected this concept?
16 How do you want to die?
17 How do you want people to remember you after you are dead?

Preparing to shoot

The primary goal was to shoot the interviews as "talking heads" and not worry so much about the B-roll (see pages 84–85) when I was there, since photos and stock footage would augment the majority of what they would talk about. I imagined most of the B-roll footage to consist of various city and nature shots.

Equipment and crew

Due to the budget and time constraints I was the only crew member, which made the planning and then shooting of the documentary entirely manageable. The documentary was shot in Standard Digital, on MiniDV cassettes, and in widescreen (16:9) format.

The equipment consisted of what was necessary to videotape the interviews—the camera, tripod, audio, and a few lights—and was primarily the same for all locations. The only difference was the transportation used: when I got to NYC, the camera was carried on the plane to prevent any damage, since it was the most important piece of equipment. The lights, light stands, cords, and camera tripod were mailed to the work location in NYC a week ahead of time, so all was ready for filming. (See pages 94–97 for shooting a documentary.) A lighter tripod and a wireless microphone were also used for the NYC shoots, since they were easier to pack and carry.

In my equipment package, I included a smaller, more manageable camera tripod with the lights. This was sent in one large box, one week ahead of time. This was transferred to a rolling, hard-backed duffel bag to make it more mobile for one person to carry.

Equipment list:

1. Sony DCR-VX2100 (Standard Digital, wide-screen) ✓
2. Fluid-head tripod ✓
3. Lights—two omni lights (for front and back light), one total light cable, stands, diffusion ✓
4. Audio—directional microphone on mic stand, or wireless microphone with cables ✓
5. Duct tape ✓
6. Extension cords ✓
7. Video tape (MiniDV) ✓

This equipment list is made with one person in mind, who will have to transport and carry it to the various interview shoots. Everything fits within two or three cases that can be hand-carried.

Transporting equipment for flight

If you can, carry on the camera and audio in an over-the-shoulder camera case. On the plane, fit this under the seat in front of you. Never let the camera out of your sight.

Transporting equipment for mailing

Remove the bulbs from the lights and protect with bubble wrap. Pack all other equipment firmly within the package—the less room there is for movement, the less likely breakages are to occur.

See what happens during the shoot, turn to page 94.

SHOOTING AND COVERAGE

The goal when shooting is to get as much coverage as possible
and to shoot as well as you can within the time allotted.

Plan your time

Give yourself plenty of time to get all of your
shots. The last thing you need on a shoot is to be
running around like a chicken without its head.
Estimate how long it will take to set up lights and
equipment at a certain location. For example, you
may be videotaping someone in their office,
which is on the first floor of a building. Getting in
will only take a few minutes. However, if you are
interviewing a doctor on the fifth floor of a
hospital, you will probably have to get through
the hospital's security, then haul the equipment
from a parking structure a distance away and up a
service elevator, so you will need to allow much
more time than with the first scenario.

You may also need to allow time to get
additional footage of the interviewee, for example
of the doctor working in his office with a patient.
You can shoot this footage on the same tape as
the interviews, making it easier to locate in post-
production. Remember, this actual production is
when you get all the raw material you need for
your documentary. You cannot edit something
together if you never shot it to begin with.

Continuity

Be consistent in your screen format and frame
speed, shooting everything in wide-screen if that
is your chosen format, or 24 frames per second if
you are going for a "film look." Changing these
around in editing can be very time-consuming.
You should also be mindful of continuity when
interviewing individuals, and try to schedule all
their shoots within a set time period. For example,
if you shoot part of an interview in the winter
when the interviewee has a beard, then shoot the
remainder of his interview in the spring when he
no longer has a beard, and sections of these
interviews are mixed in editing, the result is
going to be very distracting to the viewer.

B-roll

If you plan to make an hour-long documentary,
you will have quite a bit of footage to shoot.
Generally, documentary shooting adheres to a
30:1 ratio, which means that for an hour-long
program, you should expect to have 30 hours or
30 one-hour tapes of footage. Two-thirds of this
will most likely be "B-roll" footage. This is the
footage that goes over the interviews. For
example, audio of a person discussing playing
soccer could be accompanied by footage of the
player at a game. Footage like this makes the
documentary more interesting, since viewers get
bored if they have to watch "talking heads" for
more than a few minutes at a time.

Scope of footage

Coverage of shots also involves getting more
than one take, such as a wide, medium, and
close-up shot of the exterior of a location, so that
you can decide which looks best later on. You may
have to stop frequently and consult your
blueprint and storyboards if you are using them.
If you are shooting a one-time event and
coverage is crucial, it may be beneficial to shoot
with more than one camera. If you do this, make
sure the cameras are comparable and their
images look similar to each other.

It is always good to have more footage than
you think you will need, so do not be timid about
getting the shots; you will often only have the
one chance.

Lesson 20 :
How to get the most production value

At the most basic level, production value is the overall quality of the film. The better or more involved something looks, the higher its production value.

KEY POINTS:
Increasing production value

> Take care with lighting your interviews.

> Use scenic locations.

> Improvise moving shots and aerial shots.

> Utilize stock footage.

● >>> **Assignment 21**

Make a list of ten things you can do that would increase the production value of your documentary.

A $100,000 production will have a higher production value than a $1,000 production, simply because it has the luxury of having more resources available. Even though your film may be far less in cost, it will still expected to have as good a production value as it can. You need to do everything you can to get the "most bang for your buck."

High value on a low budget

To create high production value with a lesser budget, first take the time to think shots out. Make sure everything is in focus, and ensure that the audio is being clearly recorded. One way to work toward better production value is to set up

better shots. Take time to think about the lighting and the shot composition of each scene before you begin shooting. Are you going to go with the acceptable fluorescent lighting in a children's activity room, or make it warmer and more inviting by using colored gels? Are you going to just show something, or make it cinematic to add to the viewing experience? By simply using stock footage, such as time-lapse photography of clouds or sunsets, you can easily enhance the production and make it seem bigger than it is.

Tip

Famous faces
Celebrities, whether they are on camera or doing narration, increase the production value of your documentary.

Tip

Moving shots
If you are shooting someone running outside or walking toward the camera and desire a smoother shot than handheld, shoot on a tripod from the open back trunk of a car. The driver will have to drive very slowly, for both you and the subject.

TECHNIQUE FILE

Maximizing production value

It's likely that you will be working with a limited budget, but regardless of your funding, there are some simple things you can do to create high value on a low budget.

1 Consider your location: *The location for your documentary can make a world of difference. Carefully chosen or scenic locations can make the production seem more expensive than its actual cost. If you have the option of videotaping a priest in an office or in a cathedral, for example, opt for the cathedral. It might mean a bit more work when it comes to setting up the equipment, but it will definitely be worth it.*

2 Take care with lighting and audio: *Lighting your subject well (to make the scene more inviting) and ensuring any sound (particularly interview conversations or narration) is clearly audible are easy ways (and musts!) to add production value to your program.*

3 Find a famous face: *Celebrities, whether they are on camera or narrating, increase the production value of your documentary.*

4 Keep it moving: *Moving shots are usually much more dynamic than static shots or camera movements, and again can make the production seem more expensive than its actual cost. Renting an expensive Steadicam to get a moving shot in a hotel may not be possible, but achieving a similarly moving shot by placing the camera on a borrowed baggage cart is a cheaper alternative.*

1 Laura Zinger interviews Amos Paul Kennedy Jr., as Michelle Kaffko shoots, for the film Proceed and Be Bold! (2008) This interview was taken in Cameri, Italy, a location that adds production value to the film.

2 Interviewee Ayo Salau-beseke talks about the differences in breastfeeding habits of Americans and Nigerians. Great care is taken in the lighting and particularly audio, as she supplies much of the information.

3 Bono appears in a shoot for Amnesty International, an organization with which he is already involved. Celebrities will often agree to be in a documentary if it is a subject/topic they support and are associated with.

Lesson 21 : Be true to your subject

The specific shots you use and how they are arranged should accurately convey what the documentary is about. Occasionally, in order to get usable footage, you have to "cheat" things, for example by restaging certain events.

> Objectives

> To ensure that the pictures and sound in the documentary represent the "truth" of the subject.
> To resort to staged shots only when it's impossible to get "real" footage of what you need.

Bending the truth

"Cheating" can be as simple as filming an individual sitting at their desk and working on their computer to get a necessary shot for when the subject is talking about their work-at-home job. They may not be working at the precise moment you are shooting them, but the shot does represent something that is true. If you are making a simple nature short about the lifespan of a frog, you could first show a frog laying eggs in a pond, then the eggs turning into tadpoles, then the tadpoles with legs, and the final frog, which then eats a dragonfly and is eaten by a heron. To illustrate this, you would probably videotape many different frogs and edit the footage together to give the impression that this is the lifespan of a single amphibian. This is all acceptable because it shows the truth of the subject matter. It doesn't have to literally be true, or be really happening then and there. The image does not have to match up exactly with what is being talked about, but the key is to not misrepresent the "reality" of the subject.

For example, if you are making a documentary about a live event, such as a pie-eating contest, you would not want to restage anything; instead, you want to capture the feel of the event as it is happening. However, if someone is talking about their emotional ups and downs while trying to

● >>> Assignment 22

Go through your blueprint to see how many sections of your documentary you will need to re-create or stage in order to get the shots you need.
Consider the first three shots you will need to create. Do these shots represent the "truth"?

get a grip on their mental illness, and you cut to footage of a roller coaster, you are giving the viewer something visual to look at, even though what the interviewee is talking about has nothing to do with roller coasters. The images help to convey that person's emotional state, and the viewer will understand that the footage is included for artistic reasons.

Re-creations

Re-creations are primarily used when footage or photos are unavailable, such as in a documentary about the Middle Ages or Vikings in America. These scenes often utilize actors and sets to stage particular events in time, set the scene, and tell the story. Historical documentaries such as these may even use clips from narrative movies to illustrate a scene, for example, showing the clip of the slaves building the pyramid in Cecil B. DeMille's *The Ten Commandments* (1956), or stop-motion dinosaurs from Irwin Allen's *The Animal World* (1956) to show what these animals may have looked like and how they would have behaved in real life.

Bias

The "truth" of your documentary is likely to depend on your subject. Showing certain facts, perhaps in a performative/expository documentary about the state of health care or the threat of global warming, can present a biased opinion. All the facts may be true, but they support the opinions and message of the documentary and its makers, and are intended to influence viewers' ways of thinking.

Left: The Animal World *(1956)*
As the filmmakers would have been hard pressed to film a living brontosaurus, it was re-created through the techniques of the time period in which it was made, namely using stop-motion animation. It is a good "guess" that the creature resembled this re-creation.

WHAT TO WATCH

Murder City, Detroit: 100 Years of Crime and Violence (2008) Directed by Al Profit, this film uses archival footage to show how Detroit transformed from a model city in the 1930s to murder capital of the world. This program emphasizes the negative aspects of the city—a good example of bias in action.

Giant Monsters (2010) Wildlife adventurer Jeff Corwin is placed alongside huge, prehistoric spiders and gigantic, carnivorous lizards. The animals are re-created through computer animation and the premise is that he's not really there; his presence is to emphasize their size and power compared to man.

An Inconvenient Truth (2006) (1) Al Gore's environmental documentary could be called "An Incomplete Truth," since it fervently sticks with one theory. Another good example of bias in action.

Bowling for Columbine (2002) (2) In this documentary, which makes a case for more gun control in the U.S., Michael Moore stays true to his subject, and doesn't shy away from the fact that he's a member of the NRA (National Rifle Association).

Life After People (2008) This film theorizes about what would happen to our planet if humans disappeared. Since time machines don't exist, many of the visuals are created with computer animation, based on the best guesswork of scientists and engineers.

Lesson 22 : Directing the documentary

As the director, you must have the answers to everything during the production of your documentary.

> Objective

> To decide how much "hands on" directing you will need to do, based on the subject and content of your documentary.

Action

Action and *cut* remain the universal film terms for "go" and "stop." Use these when you are videotaping so people know that you are recording.

● >>> Assignment 23

Go through your script or documentary outline and anticipate how much of your documentary will require you to direct your subjects and situations.

Directing a documentary doesn't involve telling people what to say, but you may be suggesting how they should say it. When the person being interviewed is asked a question, you may want them to incorporate it in their answer, especially for reference. For example, if you ask them the question, "When was the first time you encountered death?", they would begin their answer with "I had my first encounter with death when I was...." You may also have to ask them the question a second time if a phone ringing in the background interrupts them, or if they are unclear in answering something you need clarified.

The director's instruction

When you are shooting other footage, such as your subject working at their job, you may direct them to walk down a hallway, or demonstrate a power tool. There may be multiple takes and different angles, which you will fit together seamlessly during editing. The viewer watching this later on will not question that they're watching something as it actually happens. In fact, before you shot anything, you may have told them to wear a suit, or just a t-shirt and jeans. You are simply getting your shots in the direction in which you need them. If you are shooting a re-creation of a scene—and are using actors to represent the individuals being discussed in the program—you will be directing them on everything from their performance to where they are standing.

If you have crew members on a shoot, you will also be directing them—from telling the camera person that you want a "medium shot" for this interview, to telling the lighting guy to put up another light because the subject has distracting shadows on their face. Be firm in your decisions but also be open to suggestions, especially if this is not your area of expertise, i.e. with the lighting. Your crew members are creative, too, and will bring their own knowledge to the shoot. It is your job as the director to bring the best out in all.

Staged performances

Directing a reenactment or scene that's set up specifically for the documentary gives you more control as a director, as opposed to shooting a live performance. It will involve everything from setting up the stage and lighting it, to instructing your talent where to stand on stage and for how long he should perform. Although you may only be using a segment of of the staged performance, it's best to record the entire thing.

Directing a staged performance
In the performance that's staged opposite, you can see:
1. The stage is set and lit well before the talent arrives. There is no need for your actors/performers to wait around while you get everything organized. This will only make them more nervous and this is the last thing you want.
2. and 3. The performer is directed to begin playing as he would in an ordinary performance. The shot begins with a wide angle, to show the context of him performing on stage, before moving in for a tighter shot until the end of the song. Again the performer is instructed to perform as he would in front of an ordinary audience; it's important that the performance doesn't appear to be staged.
4–8. The performer is having to "fend for himself" from lack of direction and is clearly ill at ease. One of your most important jobs as director is to make your subjects comfortable. Giving the sense that you are in control of your production only succeeds in making the production go more smoothly.

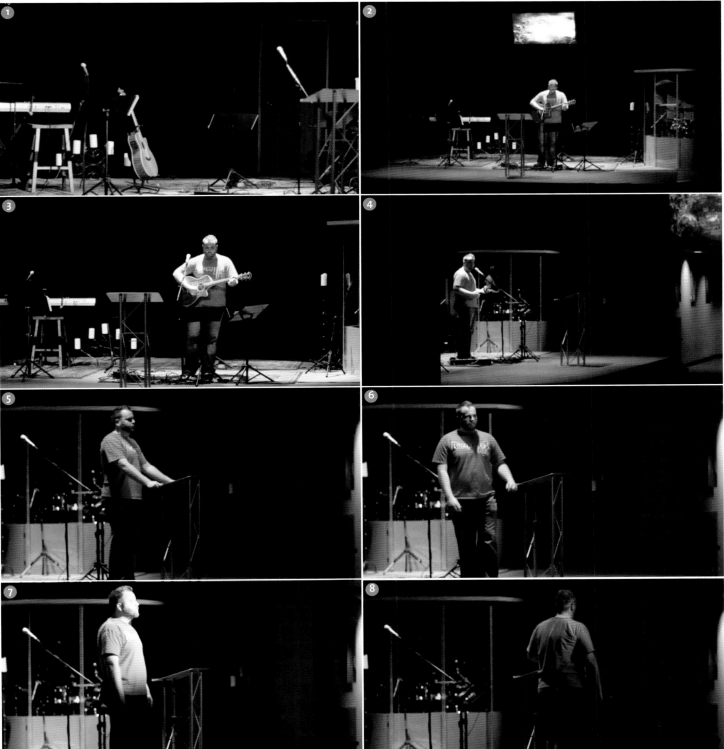

Lesson 23 : Getting enough B-roll

The B-roll is the interesting visual footage that is used to embellish interviews. To ensure you have enough B-roll, always shoot far more footage than you will need. When it comes time to edit, having more than enough leaves you in a much better position than not having sufficient footage.

> **Objective**

> To establish how much B-roll footage you might need, and in what form.

● >>> **Assignment 24**

Skip to three different chapters of a documentary DVD, and watch five minutes of each to ascertain how the B-roll complements the storyline. Why does it work? Do the images literally go with the voice-over/narration, or do they emotionally augment it?

Now go through your blueprint and make a list of all the types of footage that will make your documentary more interesting to the viewer. Does the footage need to be literal or abstract, according to the style of the documentary?

When in doubt, keep the camera rolling; you can never shoot too much. However, don't be alarmed if you discover in editing that you still need to shoot additional B-roll footage.

Relevant B-roll
At the time of shooting interviews, also try to capture as much of the surroundings as you can. This could be the objects on the interviewee's desk, or on their bookshelves, or them looking out of the window. This way, when you are editing, you can visually stay in that same space without having to cut to something unrelated to these surroundings. Get as much as you can of the person on location, perhaps walking, sitting on a park bench, or playing with their children, if it's relevant.

If it's not possible to get additional footage of these things then and there, schedule a day in which you can visit the interviewee with the specific purpose of getting various B-roll shots. It may be easier for you to do this after you have shot and watched the interview footage, since you can videotape activities or objects that are relevant to what was said on the first tape. You may also want to have the interviewee change clothes a few times, to give the impression that they were shot over the course of a few days.

Abstract B-roll
If there is no obvious B-roll for what you are shooting, for example, a person relating an emotional experience that happened in their past, be creative. This can be as basic as using

B-roll in adbundance
Over 800 hours of footage was shot for Where in the World is Osama Bin Laden *(2008). The majority of this was for B-roll footage.*

footage of a flower or sunrise to represent life or happiness, or a fall leaf or bleak landscape to convey loneliness or isolation. The B-roll doesn't literally have to be what is being talked about. It is used to help convey the idea of your documentary and add to the viewer's understanding.

Photographs

It may not be possible for you to shoot the B-roll you need, particularly if the documentary is about past events. If you think you may need photographs from an interviewee, ask them to bring them to the shoot that day or to mail them to you. If they are old prints you may have to videotape them or scan them into your computer so you can use them in editing. Old home videos are also useful.

Edits

B-roll footage serves a practical purpose in the editing suite, in covering the edits you make with the interviews. When editing a sentence here, taking out an "um" or a cough there, rather than having an abrupt jump cut, you can use B-roll footage to hide the edit. While you could dissolve from the same medium shot of a person to them later on in the conversation, most times this does not look very good and is distracting. However, if the interviewee is talking about their childhood house, showing video or photos of that actual house covers up the jump edits.

Make it relevant
Make sure, when using photos, that you choose ones that fit the content of your documentary. As sentimental as the images shown left are, it makes no sense to include such childhood snippets if no references are made to childhood in the film.

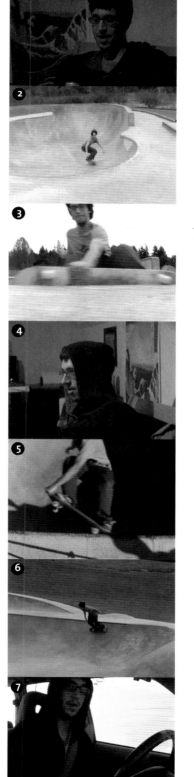

Fleshing out the story
In this documentary on skateboarding, the B-roll footage of various skateboarding moves (2,3,5, and 6) is used to augment the interview with the skateboarder. As this is a very visual activity, it's a must to show what the interviewee is talking about (in 1, 4, and 7). All of the B-roll footage shown was shot on a different day, after the main interview, so the filmmaker knew exactly what type of shots were needed. For added effect, the interview footage was made black and white in editing, to convey the feeling that "real life" is less colorful than when pursuing the passion of skateboarding.

KEY POINTS: Deciding what kind of B-roll footage you need

> What images do you need to tell the story?
> What images are available to shoot?
> Do your images need to be literal or abstract?
> What footage might you have to shoot last?

Lesson 24 :
Shooting techniques

The manner in which you shoot and light your documentary can have a tremendous effect on the viewer.

> **Objective**
> To decide ahead of time the types of shot and camera angles you will use consistently throughout the production.

Moving the camera, such as panning with a jogger, gives the impression of movement. A tilt down from the sky to a park will effectively establish a new location. Shooting the passing landscape from the window of a car implies travel or time passing. A handheld, "shaky" camera during a sporting event may heighten the action. You may even choose to do something unexpected, such as shooting a group of children from a low angle, so that the viewer is looking up at them. Would this make viewers identify with them more since they are not looking down at them? Whatever you choose, make sure there is a good reason for being creative with your shots.

The 180-degree rule

The 180-degree rule simply states that, to avoid confusing the viewer, you should always stay on the same side of the subject you are shooting. For example, when filming a boy and girl playing on a swing set, with the boy on the left and the girl on the right, you can still move around and change the camera angle, as long as you remain on the same side of the children, so that the boy stays on the left and the girl on the right. If you hop over to the other side, you change their orientation, which makes for very jolting and confusing footage.

CORRECT
Pick a side and stay with it, always remembering that if someone is on the left side of the screen they need to be on the left in the next shot as well. For reverse-angle shots in an interview, the camera placement will be on the top and bottom of the half circle.

INCORRECT
You want your audience to have a consistent position when watching your documentary. If shooting on the right side of the circle, you cannot take your camera to the other side as this will cause the characters to switch places on the screen, and your footage will not cut together in editing.

Point-of-view shot
The only way to see through the eyes of this motorcycle rider is from the back seat, shooting with a handheld camera at a high angle. It is an exciting POV (point-of-view) shot.

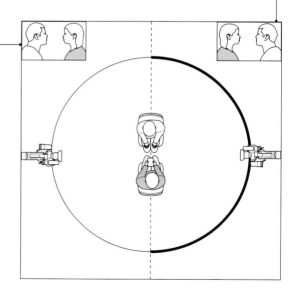

Deciding on shots and angles

Take a look at the shots and angles below. Which do you think will work well in your documentary? Keep in mind that often many of the shots and angles listed below may be combined.

1 Extreme long shot: *This shot usually establishes the setting, such as a town or a tropical island, to give an impression rather than specific detail, and can be from miles away.*

2 Long shot: *When filming a person, this shot shows their entire body and the setting. Also called a "wide shot."*

3 Medium shot: *This captures a person from the waist up, and is especially useful if the person gestures a lot. Also called a "mid-shot."*

4 Close-up: *Generally, this shot shows a person from the chest up, and is particularly good for intimate interviews.*

5 Extreme close-up: *Used to show specific detail, this shot encompasses just the person's face, or perhaps just their hands.*

6 Bird's-eye view: *Useful when you want to depict the layout of a location, such as a race track, this shot shows a person from above and a distance away, looking straight down on them from a stationary position.*

7 High-angle shot: *Not as high or as distant as the bird's-eye view, a high-angle shot looks slightly down at a subject. If this is a person, it usually signifies that they are feeling vulnerable and overwhelmed.*

8 Low-angle shot: *The low-angle shot looks at the subject from below, and is used for interviews, especially with "experts," to make them seem powerful or in control.*

9 Eye-level shot: *The camera is at the same level as the subject, usually during an interview.*

10 Tilted angle: *Here, the camera is at an angle to the subject. If a person is shot this way, it's to signify uneasiness or tension.*

11 Pan: *This is the sideways camera movement, right to left or left to right.*

12 Tilt: *This is the up-and-down camera movement, such as showing the sky then moving down to show a house.*

13 Dolly shot: *This is a smooth, moving shot. The camera and tripod are usually set on a stand-alone rolling platform (doorway dolly) or a platform that uses tracks, like a miniature train.*

14 Crane shot: *The camera is mounted at the end of a crane, which is controlled by a person at the other end. An example is beginning from a bird's-eye point of view then moving down to eye level.*

15 Aerial shot: *Similar to the bird's-eye view, only moving; for example, a shot of a city, filmed from a helicopter.*

Extreme long shot

Crane/dolly shot

High-angle shot

Dolly shot

Eye-level shot

Aerial shot

Low-angle shot

Extreme close-up

Directing the viewer

To establish a location, you may begin with an extreme long shot of the skyline of a city, then cut to a long shot of a specific building, followed by a medium shot of the front entranceway of that building. These three different shots, each one progressively closer, direct the viewer to the location.

Emotion

A slow camera zoom is particularly effective when shooting an emotional interview. Start off on the standard medium shot, then, when the interview becomes more poignant or moving, slowly zoom in to a more intimate close-up of the face of the interviewee. By zooming in on the speaker, you are physically and emotionally bringing the viewer closer to your subject.

CONTINUITY

● *Continuity mistakes can be distracting to your viewer. For example, if you are interviewing a subject who's sitting in front of a wall clock, make sure to stop that clock or simply remove it from the shot. If someone is sitting down, drinking a glass of water, and the glass is in the frame, make sure it's always filled to the same amount or else it will be noticeable that the level goes up and down, since you may not edit the interview clips in the order they were shot.*

The woman being interviewed here is holding her baby in this documentary about breast-feeding.

As the subject of this documentary is the commercial airplane that crashed into the Hudson River, the wide shot (1) establishes the context, then moves in (2) and closes in on the vehicle (3).

Here, parents talk about the health of their children (1), zooming first on the mother (2), then panning to the father when he talks (3). These close-up shots give an intimate feel to the documentary and make the story all the more personal.

Here, she continues the discussion alone. Also note that she is sitting in a different chair.

TECHNIQUE FILE

In-camera transitions

You can use your camera to create edit points for specific shots. For example, to establish a location during a certain time of day, show the sky, then tilt down to show a house below; or have someone in the distance walk toward the camera so that eventually their body blocks the camera lens and light, creating a physical "fade to black." Another simple transition is to do a "rack focus"—change the focus from an object in the background to an object in the foreground, for example, to show a bug on a leaf.

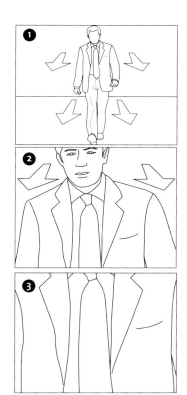

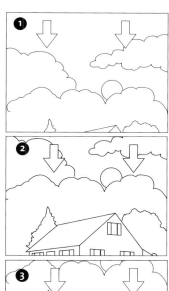

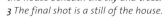

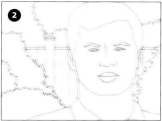

Person walking into camera
1 The person, in the distance, walks directly toward the camera.
2 The person gets closer, not looking at the camera.
3 The person appears as if they "walk into" the camera at chest level.

Camera tilts down
1 A still, wide shot of the sky and tops of the trees tilts down after a few seconds.
2 The camera is tilting down, revealing the house beneath the sky and trees.
3 The final shot is a still of the house.

Rack focus
1 The background foliage is in focus, and the man is not.
2 Neither the background or the foreground is in focus.
3 The man in the foreground is now in focus and the background is out of focus.

Get your lighting right

Avoid high-contrast lighting, such as shooting someone in a room against an open window—unless you only wish to see their silhouette, which may be appropriate if they want to remain anonymous. Instead, make sure the strongest lighting is directed on the person.

Make sure nothing in the shot is overexposed, such as a lamp in the corner or a glare from the light on a white wall,

since this will look sloppy and indicate that you didn't take the time to set the shot right. Many cameras have a "zebra function," (see page 44) which shows whether an image is overexposed in the form of lines crossing the image. The rule of thumb is that it is better to be underexposed than overexposed, because you can always brighten the levels. You cannot undo levels if they are too high; the image will still appear overexposed.

(see page 44)

> > > **Assignment 25** ●

Considering the key points above, go through several pages of your blueprint and/or script and write down what angles and shots you will use in that section.

Lesson 25 : Wardrobe, makeup, and props

In a documentary, wardrobe takes precedence over makeup. You want your interviewee to look as natural as possible and be wearing what they would normally wear.

Keeping it real
You won't be able to input on makeup and wardrobe for spontaneous interviews, but at least they will be "real."

Objective
> To make sure your interviewees are wearing clothes that represent their role in the documentary.

● >>> **Assignment 25**

Imagine you are interviewing a grandfather, a teenaged girl, and a computer scientist. What would you tell each of them to wear for their interview?

Wardrobe

When planning your interviews, ask people what they are likely to wear, and advise them of the types of clothing they should avoid.

Make sure that the clothes are not too contrasting. For example, a vertically striped shirt will seem to shimmer on video. This is distracting to the viewer. Also, if you are shooting someone against a white wall, make sure they are not wearing black, because black absorbs light and will make the wall seem brighter. Conversely, if they are wearing black and being shot against a black background, they may look like a disembodied head.

What the interviewee wears must also identify them. If you are interviewing a farmer about some aspect of his crops, you do not want him wearing a three-piece suit. Likewise, a funeral director would not wear denim suspenders and a baseball cap, and a doctor would most likely wear his white lab coat.

Makeup: Practicality vs. necessity

Man-on-the-street interviews may be spontaneous, in which case you may have no control over makeup or wardrobe. However, you may be searching for people with a certain "look," depending upon your subject matter. Women will tend to do their own makeup. The most you may need to do is cover up a few zits. Makeup generally makes men uncomfortable, unless they are television professionals. It's not good to make your interviewee uncomfortable on camera, so it may be best to forego any makeup. That said, you may have to give someone's bald spot less glare with a flat, base makeup, which can be purchased online through any video production store.

For a low-budget production in which you cannot afford to pay anyone, you're not likely to find a professional makeup artist who will work for free or for a credit. If you absolutely need a makeup artist, hire a professional just for the days you will need them.

Identify your interviewee
Advise your interviewee about what they should wear and make sure their clothing helps to identify them. In this case (right), Dr. Ben Song talks about the medical symptoms of having an anaphylactic reaction. Although it may be somewhat stereotypical, the lab coat and stethoscope immediately tell the viewer that this is the "expert."

TECHNIQUE FILE

Getting it right

Clothing, makeup, and props for an individual in your documentary are not as much of a necessity as they would be for a Hollywood actor, but if you want your documentary to be taken seriously and look professional, these are things you should consider. When deciding on how far to go with your wardrobe, makeup, and props, you might need some help. Different scenes, and indeed different documentaries, will require different makeup applications, but here are just a few basic points to help you on your way.

Tip

Use the camera as your makeup assistant
Lighting and camera angles can be used wisely to make the most of a person's appearance. When working with a person who is overweight, shooting slightly down on them straight on can make it look like they have double chins, so shoot them slightly from the side and from below. Similarly, lighting can get rid of shadows that will otherwise make a person look tired or unhealthy.

1 Keep it real: For a realistic, slice-of-life documentary (particularly where man-on-the-street interviews are concerned) you should strive to represent the "everyday person," especially if it's about a broad topic. A makeup artist is not usually necessary, since you are shooting your subject "as is," not trying to make them look like a different person. Your goal is to have them appear as natural as possible (as shown on the left)—i.e., how they would normally look.

2 Special effects: If you are doing a reenactment of a scene, you may need to deal with special effects and props. Here, filmmaker John Borowski applies blood to the actor who portrays the title character in H.H. Holmes: America's First Serial Killer (2004). If you are doing a reenactment and need to create something much more complicated, for example, burn wounds for a documentary about firefighters, you need to find an artist proficient in makeup effects. In both instances, be sure to have paper towels handy, since the lights are hot and people will sweat.

3 Use props: Take advantage of props that fit the scene, as they can make shots more visually interesting. Here, a young girl tries to manage using an umbrella in the rain. The shot is used as B-roll over an interview of the girl's mother talking about her child's health condition, which fits with the film and endears the girl to the viewer.

Lesson 26 : The setup for sit-down interviews

When setting up to videotape an interview, arrive at least one hour before your scheduled shoot, giving yourself plenty of time to set up your equipment.

> ## > Objectives
> > To plan in advance how to get all your questions answered.
> > To plan how you are going to shoot the sequence.

KEY POINTS: Setting up

> Give yourself plenty of time to set up the equipment for the interview.
> Make the interviewee comfortable.
> Have the subject look off to one side of the camera when answering questions.
> Make sure you see "light in their eyes."
> Ensure that there are no "hot spots" from overexposure.
> Keep the camera rolling the entire time you do the interview.

● > > > Assignment 26

Pick two different individuals you think you will interview for your documentary. For each of them make a checklist of all the specifics you want to accomplish, such as determining where you want to shoot the interview, what the setting and tone is, and whether you are going to have them look to the right or left of the camera. Be as detailed as possible.

Once you are in the location, whether it be an office or a room in a house, decide where you are going to sit your interviewee. Avoid windows and try not to have too much clutter in the background. You also do not want to shoot against a blank wall.

Frame

When taping, you should be framing the subject's head and shoulders with a medium shot. If they use their hands a lot when talking, you may want to stay on this medium shot and make sure you capture the gestures. At certain points you may want to zoom in for a closer, more intimate shot, especially if they are talking about something personal or emotional.

Questioning

Your subject may be nervous at first, particularly if they've never been in front of a camera, so aim to make them feel as comfortable as possible. After 10 or 15 minutes, even the most nervous subject tends to forget about the camera because they are focused on the interviewer. Sometimes you will have to repeat those first few questions at the end of the interview to get better answers. During all of this, keep the camera rolling. When asking the questions, have the subject repeat the question as a statement, which will help immensely when you get to editing the footage. Afterward, you may want to videotape the subject for some B-roll footage, such as them working in their office or walking outside.

POSITIONING

● *Sit your subject 6–8 feet (1.8–2.4 m) from the camera, which should be level or a little lower than the person, so you are not looking down on them. However, you want to avoid the "double-chin effect" from having the camera placement too low. Once your subject is seated, make the necessary adjustments, ensuring that nothing unusual is happening in the shot, such as a lamp or a plant seemingly growing out of the subject's head.*

● *When asking the questions, sit either to the right or left of the camera (it's good to vary this if you are doing a lot of interviews) so that when the interviewee answers, they look at you and not the camera.*

● *If you are doing the camerawork yourself, find someone else to sit in the chair and ask the questions, though it is possible to do both if need be.*

Lighting your interview

You will need a minimum of two lights for an interview.

The first is a **key light***, in front, usually behind the camera and interviewer. Make sure you can see the light in the subject's eyes, since it makes them more "alive," and avoid casting shadows that crease the face.*

A **back light** *is set off behind the interviewee, to the side, to cast light on the back of their head and separate them from the background. You may also choose to have a third* **fill light** *in the front and on the other side of the key light to get rid of any shadows.*

The illustration on the right shows the perfect lighting setup for an interview, and the photos below show the effects each light provides.

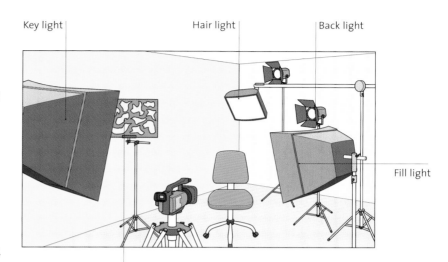

Key light   Hair light   Back light

Fill light

Cucoloris or gobo, a device used for casting shadows and silhouettes.

Lighting effects (from left to right):
1 Key light: *Puts the focus directly on the subject—can make the subject look "in the spotlight."*
2 Hair light: *This setup creates a somber effect.*
3 Backlight: *Moody, dramatic effects can be generated with back lighting.*
4 Fill light combined with key, back, and hair lights: *The most even "all-over" lighting.*

Case study: *Shooting a documentary*

Following on from the planning stages for the documentary *The Life Of Death* (see pages 72–75), Kevin Lindenmuth continues his account of the shooting process. The crux of the documentary lies in what the individuals say; B-roll is a secondary concern and will be dealt with during post-production (see pages 134–135), since this will primarily include personal photos and stock footage. The main logistical factor with this project is that Kevin will be doing all of the work, and is trying to do it as inexpensively as possible.

Interview timings
By the time pre-production was completed, there were thirteen interviewees and it was estimated that each interview would take between 45 minutes and one hour, with 30 minutes to set up, and 30 minutes to pack up the equipment. With the addition of traveling time, this would mean spending 3–5 hours per interview, or half a day.

The setup for the interviews
This was a "one-man-band" project: as producer/director, I'd also be shooting the interviews and asking the questions. All of the interviews had to look consistent in how they were lit and

arranged, so a simple setup was decided upon. While setting up the lights, camera, and audio, I would talk with the interviewee and warm him or her up. I'd set the camera frame and sit to the right of the camera, so I could also look at the pop-out screen. On average, this would take 2–3 hours of time per interviewee, which translated to one or two 60-minute digital tapes of footage.

Style
The premise was that these varying individuals would be candidly talking about their views on what many consider to be a taboo subject, almost as if the viewer were having an intimate conversation with them. They were all seated and talking to one side of the camera, while I, as producer, was seated and asking the questions. The interviewees were asked to incorporate the questions into their answers, to make editing more cohesive. Most of the interviews would be shot in a medium shot, though there were to be close-ups on some of the more emotional answers.

Filming the interviews
With the Michigan interviews there was no time constraint. There was plenty of time to drive out, set up the equipment,

and do the interviews. None of the locations were previously scouted. They were in three completely different locations: a church, an office, and a house. The New York City interviews were all shot in offices and apartments. Key points of a selection of the interviews are documented below.

Backup equipment
Wireless lavalier microphones are notorious for getting static interference, particularly if you are shooting in a city with tall buildings. This can be caused by anything from the steel girders in the structure to radio waves and microwaves. For this reason, always have a backup microphone that plugs directly into your camera. Cables can also break, so keep an extra ten-foot (3 m) audio cable as well. Extra batteries are also a must.

Caring for equipment in the cold
If you are shooting during the winter, never leave your camera outside or in your automobile for any length of time. Cold air sucks energy out of the camera batteries, and there is also the problem of condensation if the camera is then brought into a heated room. Leave the cold camera inside for 30 minutes to allow it to "warm up" before use. Similarly, if lights get too cold the bulbs may explode if plugged in right away, so allow 30 minutes for them to reach room temperature.

Diagram for shooting

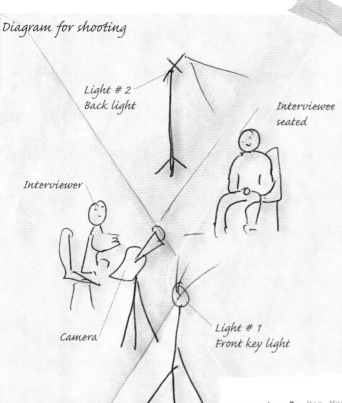

Light # 2
Back light

Interviewee
seated

Interviewer

Camera

Light # 1
Front key light

Two lights were used for these interviews since only medium shots and close-ups were needed. Their location is not that important.

Plan your lighting

If you are both shooting and interviewing, a two-light setup is best, since you'll probably be pressed for time. Make sure to vary your shots in between questions and listen to the audio with a pair of headphones. Wear the headphones while you are doing the interview.

Interview 1: David Crumm, spiritual journalist.
Location: Large church in Ann Arbor, Michigan; shot in a room in front of a stained glass window and then sitting in one of the pews with ornate woodwork in background. David frequently works at the church, so obtaining permission was not an issue.
Lighting: It is overcast, so incoming daylight is manageable and does not affect production lights.
Audio: Interviewee fitted with wireless lavalier microphone.
Angle/shot: Varied; from medium shots to close-ups, depending on how emotional the answers are.
B-roll: No B-roll shot. What David speaks of is fairly abstract or about a specific experience; pictures will be used during editing to supplement.
Time at location: Three and a half hours.
Footage recorded: One and a half hours of tape.

David Crumm

Interview 2: Don May, the president of the DVD distribution company Synapse Films.
Location: Michigan. Office first, then moved to conference room because of noise level.
Lighting: Conference room is bare, with white walls. To infuse a little color, a red gel—appropriate for a horror-movie distributor—is placed over a third light and its barn doors are closed just enough to allow a slant of light to hit the wall behind the interviewee.
Audio: Interviewee fitted with wireless lavalier microphone.
Angle/shot: Varied; from medium shots to close-ups.
B-roll: Filmed Don working at his desk and examples of poster and box art from the movies the company distributes. Additional B-roll shot later in the year at the local horror movie convention.

The interviews

Here and on the next page are samples of logistical notes based on a selection of the interviews.

Don May

Continued on next page

Interview 3: Art Regner, Detroit area radio and sportscaster personality.
Location: Art's home (in the living room, most space), Michigan.
Lighting: Art filmed sitting on end of the couch with a front fill light and a smaller backlight. Sunlight was coming in through the curtained window, but as it was an overcast day, it doesn't overpower the halogen video lights.
Audio: Interviewee fitted with wireless lavalier microphone.
Angle/shot: Primarily medium shots and close-ups since he has one of the more emotional stories for the documentary.
B-roll: No B-roll is shot. Art talked about the experience he had with his sister's death, and a note is made to obtain photographs of her during editing.

Art Regner

Interviews 12 and 13: Actress Caroline Munro (*The Spy Who Loved Me, Golden Voyage Of Sinbad, Maniac*) and artist Tom Sullivan (*Evil Dead*), guests at the Cinema Wasteland Convention, Cleveland, Ohio.
Location: Hotel in Cleveland, a three-hour drive from my base. Mirrors or paintings bolted to every wall would have to be in the background no matter what angle is used, and a couch, two lamps, a small table, and a heavy wooden desk have to be moved to make space for the lights, camera, tripod, and the interviewees. Tom is interviewed that first night, in front of the curtained window. Caroline is interviewed first thing the following morning, sitting in a chair against the red wall of the room, wearing black, so the color scheme was good. It is similar to the color scheme of Sasha Graham's interview.
Lighting: Front light and back light.
Audio: The air-conditioning unit is shut off and the small refrigerator unplugged so background noise is not picked up by the microphone.
Angle/shot: Primarily medium and close-ups.
B-roll: Caroline and Tom are filmed signing autographs and meeting fans at the convention.

Interview 4: Lloyd Kaufman, president of Troma Films.
Location: Troma office, New York. This proves to be rather sparse, so the interview is set up at Lloyd's huge desk, which is covered with props from many of his movies, in particular the latex monster chickens and victims from *Poultrygeist*.
Lighting: There's light coming in through a side window, which can't be closed, as well as fluorescent lights in the ceilings. A front key light and a backlight are used in addition.
Audio: Wireless microphone.
Angle/shot: More medium shots, to include many of the props on his desk.
Special: First, Lloyd is in the "persona" he uses in his films and convention appearances—a kind of wacky screwball. It takes a good half-hour before he warms up and is himself, so several of the earlier questions are asked again to obtain more serious answers to those emotional questions.
B-roll: Film is shot of Lloyd interacting with his workers and in his editing suite. Shots are also taken of more props, box art, and posters for Troma's many films.

Lloyd Kaufman

Tom Sullivan

Production value and B-roll

On one hand this was a minimalist, bare-bones documentary production and was not cinematic. The main production value is the interviewees themselves, since talking about this particular subject, on tape, is a first for many. I had extensive stock footage of New York City, with crowds of people walking, which would further add to the scope. There were also stock nature shots, such as clouds, the sun, and the moon. When they were talking about their childhood experiences or specific people who had died, photos would be used. The exact nature of these photos and what is needed would not be certain until the footage was looked at and transcribed in post-production (see pages 134–135). Also, clips from other films and illustrations from the artists/ special effects guys would add further production value to the documentary.

Non-specific B-roll in NYC

A day was spent simply shooting "NYC people shots," such as crowds walking down streets and throngs of people in the redesigned Times Square area, in every style, from slightly out-of-focus "artsy" shots to just showing close-ups of endless pairs of feet walking by. This would add further production value to the documentary.

B-roll is the secondary footage that visually shows what the documentary is about.

Caroline Munro

Be prepared for the unexpected
When filming you may have to deal with things beyond your control. Your interviewee may have an indoor cat that insists on getting in the shot, for example, yet when the cat is put in another room, it starts meowing. The same goes for dogs, which may be barking if they are put outside. Young children are another matter entirely. In city apartments, there is everything from noisy neighbors in the hallway to sirens on the streets and airplanes flying overhead. Factors such as these may mean you have to stop and start over.

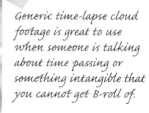

Generic time-lapse cloud footage is great to use when someone is talking about time passing or something intangible that you cannot get B-roll of.

See what happens during post-production, turn to page 134.

EDITING AND POST-PRODUCTION

Editing video is just as important as shooting video, and it is during this process that the majority of the creativity comes into play. There are two aspects to editing: the technical and the creative. Technically, you must know how to use your editing program so you can easily put scenes together; exactly how you put them together is the artistic part.

The director's intention

When you were shooting your footage everything was linear, i.e., in order. In editing you can give different meanings to a sequence simply by rearranging particular shots. What you bring to the process is your vision for the documentary. If you gave five different editors the same raw footage and told them to edit together a five-minute scene, you would be left with five different videos. This is why it is extremely important that you maintain your objective for the project, and are not overwhelmed by how easily non-linear editing enables you to change things around. First, put together a sequence the way you feel is right, going with your gut instinct. If it doesn't work you can experiment and see what works better. Good editing choices often come about in the editing process, not from your script or blueprint. Remember, be patient, since editing is a process that takes time and consideration.

The importance of good footage

Editing is not a safety net. Do not think you can necessarily correct bad video or bad audio in post-production. Color correction is also a big time-eater that does not always work. If you forgot to white-balance an inside shot and everything has a blue tinge to it because of the daylight coming in through the windows, you may be able to make the room look less blue, but perhaps at the expense of natural skin colors—especially if the scene features people with opposite skin types.

CONTENTS

Lesson 27 : **Deciding on length**

A documentary can be any length, from a five-minute short to a miniseries. While the length of your film should be enough to adequately cover your subject, the other most prominent factor is where you envision the film being seen.

> **Objective**
> > To determine how long your documentary needs to be, based on various factors.

If your film is to be entered into film festivals, do your research and find out the length requirement for submissions. If you envision it broadcasting on television, 30 minutes to 1 hour is the norm. If you are selling a DVD directly to individuals or libraries, you will be looking at 60 to 90 minutes. If you are simply posting it up on a shared video site for free, the maximum is ten minutes, unless you break it up into segments.

Whatever the length of your documentary, make sure it tells the story you intend.

Pre-production considerations
The length of your documentary should be in the back of your mind from pre-production, influencing how much footage you shoot during the actual production. If the documentary is going to be only half an hour, you probably don't need to shoot 50 hours of footage. Conversely, if you are making a feature-length film, ensure that you shoot plenty of footage to choose from.

Ask yourself if there is enough information about your subject to warrant making the documentary the length you intend. Alternatively, perhaps the subject is so all-encompassing that you need to narrow it down to a specific aspect in order to fit your desired length.

A longer documentary will cost more to produce. There is more time involved, more footage to shoot, and more tape required to record on. Then, with more footage, more hard-drive space is necessary for transferring to your editing system. Ultimately, there are more choices to make and, of course, the challenge is to keep the viewer interested for the whole film.

If you are scripting the documentary, a page of script usually equals one minute on screen, so the number of pages of script serves as a good estimate of your final length.

Editing time
The length of the documentary will also affect how much time you need to spend in editing. With a feature-length program you will have much more material to go through than with an hour-long video. If the film is intended for multiple markets, such as a film festival and then television, you will need to make two versions, each of a different length. In this instance, always edit the longer version first, since it is far easier to take away footage than to add to it.

KEY POINTS: Determining the length
> Gather all your shot tapes together and write down how many hours of footage you have to work with.
> Establish how often you have access to the editing equipment.
> List the times you are available to edit.
> Determine when you want the project completed.

● >>> **Assignment 27**

Go through your pre-production materials. Pick a page from a script or your notes and time how long it takes to read aloud. Write this down and then multiply it by how many pages you have. How many minutes are there in total?

Lesson 28 : Editing: How long will it take?

Take ample time to edit your project, but do give
yourself a specific deadline to work toward.

> ## Objective

> To establish how long it will
take you to edit your film;
give yourself a realistic
deadline to complete by.

SET A DEADLINE

● *No matter how much you plan,
editing will always take longer
than you think, so set yourself a
goal date to have the film
completed by.*

● *This deadline will help keep you
on schedule. Most importantly, it
will give you an end in sight.*

● *Editing for months at a time
can seem endless, and it is
important to keep your
enthusiasm for the project alive.*

Allocating time

For each minute of screen time there is anywhere
from three to five hours of editing involved. If
your documentary is only 30 minutes in length,
the editing time would take up about four
40-hour weeks. Editing for 10 to 15 hours per
week is realistic and manageable, particularly if
you have a full-time job. If you can put in more
time that's great, and it will only get done sooner.
The important thing is to be consistent and put
in that steady work time. This will keep the
project fresh in your mind. Instead of having to go
back and rewatch everything after a month's
hiatus, you will be able to pick up where you left
off only two days before.

   If you are editing by yourself, you only have
your own schedule to worry about. If you are
working with an editor, particularly on their
system, you may have to work to two people's
schedules. As a rule, the more people involved
with the editing, the longer it will take, primarily
because you will stop and talk about the project.

The methodical approach

For the first few weeks you may simply be
transferring selected footage onto the editing
system. While somewhat tedious, this task will
make you more familiar with your project.

   Once you are in the midst of editing you may
discover that you need to shoot additional
material. If it's primarily B-roll that you need,
make a list of the specific shots as you go along.
Once the list is complete, aim to get all the
shots done on the same day, and quickly get
back to editing.

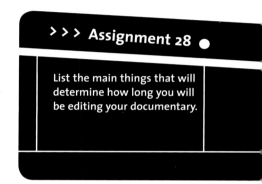

> > > **Assignment 28** ●

List the main things that will
determine how long you will
be editing your documentary.

Work out a plan
*If two or more individuals are editing the documentary,
make sure to work out an editing plan ahead of time.
Will you be working together the entire time or working
separately because of a conflict of schedules?*

Lesson 29 : **Structuring the documentary**

There are several ways to structure a documentary. The structure can be considered ahead of shooting, in production, or at the start of the editing process. If the structure of the film has not been at the front of your mind until now, it is essential that you work it out before you begin editing, otherwise you will feel as if you are endlessly juggling random footage.

> ### Objective
>
> > To determine the structure of your documentary before you begin editing.

Structuring in context
Below are four stills representative of the structure of the documentary The Basement *(2009), where artist and playwright Darrell Fusaro returns home to New Jersey to retrace the leads from the unsolved brutal mafia-style slaying of his beloved grandfather, union official James Fusaro.*

Whichever way you choose to structure your documentary, make sure that you go with your instincts. This is your project, and no one knows how to put it together better than you.

Beginning, middle, and end

The beginning and end of the documentary are what viewers will likely remember the most, so they need to make a big impression through content and editing. The beginning quickly informs your viewer what the focus of the documentary is about, and its purpose is to hook them into watching the rest of the program. The ending sums up the entire film and presents a definite message/conclusion. Remember that

while you are depicting something that is true, you are still telling a story, and all stories have a beginning, a middle, and an end. The same is true of a film, regardless of whether it is five minutes or two hours long.

At the beginning of the documentary, the viewer is presented with the subject and introduced to the characters. This is also when an emotional tie is established to an idea, object, person, or animal. If the whole film features interviews with various people, it is best to show the people—however briefly—during this time, so the viewer becomes familiar with them. Showing a few faces now, then cutting to someone completely new toward the end, will

Decades after his grandfather's murder, playwright Darrell Fusaro revisits his childhood home (production still).

Darrell describes the devastating impact the unsolved murder had on his family to the camera.

Beginning: *10–25% of the program is dedicated to the introduction—providing the background for the viewer.*

Middle: *50–80% of the documentary carries the core information, in which the filmmaker conveys the key points or message of the program, reeling the viewer in.*

seem abrupt, since the viewer will wonder where this person has suddenly come from.

During the middle part of the documentary, the bulk of the information is delivered and the topic is explored. This section could take up as much as 60 percent of the program's total running time. Ensure that your story is compelling, because it is during this section that people can get bored and tune out. Ask yourself what confrontations, conflicts, or answers need to be shown.

At the end of the documentary, wrap up the story and bring it to a conclusion by answering questions and resolving situations. In many societal-themed documentaries this may mean convincing someone that a certain viewpoint is correct. Whatever the ending is, it must sum up your intent and be satisfying to your viewer.

However, having a beginning, middle, and end does not mean that the documentary has to unfold in a sequential order. It simply has to contain these three points. For example, if you are making a documentary about the unsolved murder of a celebrity, your goal may be to present possible theories of who did it and why. Because of this you would most likely begin with the murder and work backward, so that the death in question "bookends" the documentary.

KEY POINTS: Structuring a documentary

> What is your story about?
> What makes this story unique?
> Does the story lend itself to something visual?
> Is there enough information available about this subject?
> How will this information be presented?
> Who are your main characters?
> What do those characters do and how do they propel the story?
> What is the message you want to convey?
> Does your ending pay off for your viewer?

> > > **Assignment 29** ●

Choose a topic and write down what you think would comprise the beginning, middle, and end of a documentary about it. Is there enough information?

Thirty years after the brutal slaying, Darrell's grandfather's blood still stains the walls inside this unassuming industrial building.

Darrell's Aunt expresses relief and gratitude to Darrell for bringing closure to their family's tragedy through his autobiographical play, The Basement.

The middle of the documentary must be compelling or else the viewer could lose interest and tune out.

End: 10–25% resolution and final message.

OFF

Structure and script

If you have scripted the documentary, then the script is the basis of your structure when editing. The editing process will involve arranging the footage to fit what is narrated or outlined by the script. You may end up changing some segments around, but that is to be expected.

Structure without a script

If the documentary is about a contest or an event that takes place within a specific time period, your footage will most likely unfold in order, and the flow of the event will establish the video's structure. The challenging part will be condensing everything down into the length you desire.

It is much more challenging to structure an unscripted documentary. Unlike a fictional movie script in which you write what you want the characters to say, you now have to edit together actual words and dialogue from the many different interviews. Where do you even begin? The best place to start is by watching all of your interviews and marking down the information that must be conveyed. Some people will say things better than others, and this is what you are looking for. If several parents are asked the same question, such as, "When did you first find out that your child had leukemia?" and one of them starts crying, it's probably a good bet that you'll be using that footage. You structure everything partly on what they say, partly on how they say it, and how they look while saying it.

When you begin the physical editing, you then put all of these interviews together and see how they connect with each other. Think of this as an organic process, forming as you go along. If you end up with several hours of everything you want to use, you need to whittle everything down until it fits the length of your program. The interviews are the basis of the structure, at which point you start utilizing your B-roll.

ALBERT FISH – Producer/Director: John Borowski – Location: Entertanium Studios

SET: JAIL CELL

SHOT:
DESCRIPTION: FISH READS BIBLE IN JAIL CELL
                        FISH SITS HUNCHED OVER READING
                        THE BIBLE WHILE HOLDING A ROSARY.
                        DARK – SHAFTS OF LIGHT – PREFER
                        SILHOUETTE.
TAKES: WS, MS, TRACKING IN
ACTOR(S):   FISH
COSTUME: GREY MAN - ?
PROPS: BIBLE, ROSARY, COT
MAKEUP: MUSTACHE

ALBERT FISH – Producer/Director: John Borowski – Location: Entertanium Studios

SET: KEDDEN APARTMENT

SHOT:
DESCRIPTION: KEDDEN WIDE
                        KEDDEN SITS ON THE EDGE OF THE
                        BED. YOUNG FISH'S HAND MOVES
                        INTO FRAME HOLDING CAT O' NINE
                        TAILS. WINDOW AS LIGHT SOURCE.
TAKES: WS STATIC – TRACK IN?
ACTOR(S):   KEDDEN, YOUNG FISH
COSTUME: KEDDEN COSTUME AND HAT, YOUNG
                        FISH COSTUME – PAINTER?
PROPS: CAT O' NINE TAILS, BED, WHITE SHEET

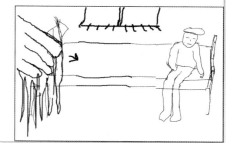

Using storyboards
Storyboards will help you structure your scripted documentary. As shown here with the storyboards from John Borowski's film Albert Fish *(2007), you will have already outlined the order, and can now edit together the real-life footage that follows it.*

WHAT TO WATCH

Grizzly Man (2005), directed by Werner Herzog, is about grizzly bear activist Timothy Treadwell who was killed in 2003 while living among grizzlies in Alaska. It uses actual footage Treadwell shot of himself, together with interviews with those who knew him. The film is structured in such a way that you have one opinion about him at the start of the film and an entirely different perspective by the time it ends. It emphasizes the plight of a misguided and ultimately, very sad, individual.

TECHNIQUE FILE

Using chapter markers

If you are producing an educational documentary intended for schools and libraries, you might organize your program by chapters or concepts. This format is useful if a documentary is to be shown in a classroom, where the audience chooses to view select portions of it. There still has to be a beginning and end to the program; however the entire middle would supply the majority of the information. Look through your documentary footage. Are there any natural points that present themselves as chapter markers? For example, if individuals are asked the same series of questions, these questions could lend themselves to actual break points in the program. Of course your chapter markers may be less obvious than this, as shown in the example below. The documentary "I'm Not Nuts": Living with Food Allergies (2009), is organized into four distinct sections, but the chapter markers are subtle, resulting in a smooth transition.

1 At the beginning, it is explained that anyone can develop a food allergy at any time in their lives. Generic B-roll of crowds of people bring this point across and earmark the first chapter which serves as an introduction.

2 The next chapter focuses on the experts. When doctors discuss the top eight foods people are allergic to, close-up shots of these food groups are used. Peanuts, while not the most prevalent, are one of the most recognized foods.

3 In the section that follows, a father calls a manufacturer to see if sesame is used, and marks the chapter in which parents discuss the safety precautions they must take, particularly in finding ingredients of food.

4 Here, parents and their children talk about how they can still enjoy food, and that children often participate in the making of family meals. This chapter marker emphasizes the "coping" element of the documentary; the child's smiling face rounds the program off on a positive note.

Lesson 30 : **Logging footage**

Logging your footage is an important part of post-production that allows you to become familiar with your material.

> **Objective**
>
> › To familiarize yourself with all of your footage and prepare for editing.

Logging is the process of organizing footage so it is ready for the edit, by means of marking down the ins and outs of the tape's time code where the specific shots are. These numbers —which show hour: minute: second: frame— provide a time reference for the non-linear editing software.

Copy for safety
To ensure that the original tapes are not damaged from overhandling, make a DVD copy of each one and log from this rather than from the tape itself. If you have a deck that can output visible or burn-

in time code on the bottom of the screen, then do that. If not, the tape's hours and minutes will roughly correspond (within 30 seconds) to the display counter of your DVD player.

Transcription and paper editing
The most thorough and time-efficient way to log interviews is to transcribe them. Write down what is said word for word, noting the time of the interview for reference. This time reference is either the counter on the DVD player or the time code if you are transcribing from the already-captured footage on your editing system. At first this may seem like a huge amount of work; however, it is distinctly preferable to scanning through video footage for hours. When all of the interviews have been transcribed,

Using still photos
If you are using still photos they will be imported from a photo program, such as Iphoto, and are usually given a default of 10 seconds, which can later be adjusted once they are placed in your editing timeline.

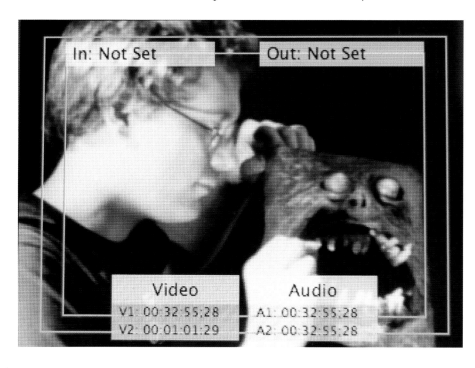

> **SMPTE TIME CODE**
>
> The standard time code for film, video, and audio is called **SMPTE time code**, established by the Society of Motion Picture and Television Engineers. It provides a time reference for editing, which lists each hour, minute, second, and frame of video, and makes video editing possible.

Keeping a log
Whether transcribing an interview or figuring the structure for your documentary, your editing process will be so much easier if you keep a log of all shots. With time codes and descriptions neatly listed in a simple form (such as that shown right), it will be much easier to locate the clips you need to transfer to your edit system.

highlight the best material; the clips that you will most likely transfer to your edit system. There is no sense inputting the entire one-hour tape if you end up using only ten select minutes from it.

If the material is from an unscripted documentary, this may be the point where you figure out the program's structure. By now you are completely familiar with what everyone says, and the links and connections between them are fresh in your mind.

When you are logging for a scripted program in which you need specific shots to match up with the prose, you need to log for those particular clips. Write this all down. Again, you do not want to load all the footage you shot into your edit system. Putting on only what you need will keep you organized and save wasted time in editing.

Making these paper edits will ensure that, further down the line, your video editing choices will be made that much easier.

The slate number is matched to the number on the shot list.

Good shots are indicated so the editor knows to ignore the ones not marked.

ROLL #	SLATE #	TAKE	TIMECODE	OK	SHOT DESCRIPTION
1	1	1	00:02		ECU OF man's face WA
		2	00:18	/	"
		3	00:35	/	"
	3	1	00:55	/	MCU of bed WA
		2	01:18		
		3	01:28	/	
		4	02:01	/	
	2	1	02:40	/	CU Girl's face WA
	4	1	04:51	/	MS overhead of bed
		2	05:24	/	
	49	1	05:57	/	MCU SLOW TRACK SHOT OF COUOR
		2	06:35	/	
	5	1	07:15	/	MC STEADICAM SHOT MC 7
		2	08:35		
		3	09:07	/	
		4	10:47	/	
	6	1	12:01	/	CU of wife
	7	1	13:24	/	MS of man preparing food
	8	1	17:51	/	CU of cereal in bowl

—72

Transcription methods
If hard drive space is not a problem, you can view all of your footage after it is captured in your editing system. Otherwise, transfer MiniDV footage to a DVD. You can then play on a DVD player and write down what the interviewee says, making necessary notes along the way.

Lesson 31 : **Where to start editing**

Now that you have logged all of your material and narrowed down your selection of usable footage, you can begin your actual editing.

● >>> **Assignment 31**

Write down three different ways in which you may approach your editing, and why they would help you.

Tip

In preparation for transitions
Always transfer at least 10–30 seconds before and after your specific shot, because you may need to add an effect over it, such as a long dissolve or a fade to black (see pages 112–113). This will use up a few unplanned seconds.

Editing begins with transferring the image and audio clips to your system and organizing the information into files, or "bins" for easy access. This may be as simple as having a separate bin for each of the interviews and one for each type of B-roll, such as "nature shots." How long the clips are and how they are divided up is entirely your choice. Just remind yourself that you need to easily access the footage when you start arranging clips in your edit timeline.

Capturing chosen footage

Begin with your first tape. Go through your log notes from beginning to end and capture each desired clip. The time code of the tapes will be visible on your capture screen when you are importing footage into your editing system. Each time you capture a specific clip, you can give it a name and save it to a specific bin. There will be

much pausing. When you have finished with that tape, put it in a safe place and move onto the next one, leaving your workspace clutter-free.

At the end of this process you may have eight to ten hours of usable footage to work with. If you later find that you need more footage, it's easy enough to go through your log shots, find what you need, and capture it.

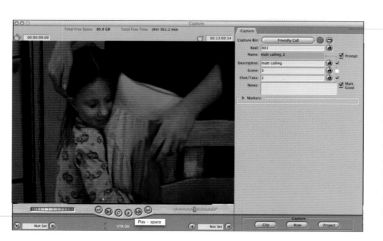

The playback source (such as camera or deck) is controlled by these buttons

Enter information about the clip in these boxes

Logging your footage
After your clips have been transferred to to your non-linear edit system, you can log information about the footage. As you can see from the Final Cut screengrab shown here, the software allows you to label all shots within a capture bin, so they can be ordered into a logical sequence later.

Deciding how to edit

You want to make editing as simple as possible when you begin. Think of your program as a body. First, you need the skeleton/structure and then you can begin adding the meat to it. Devise your editing into a series of steps so you do not get overwhelmed, then decide on your approach.

Work in order: *If your documentary is structured in a linear way, it may be best to start at the beginning and decide on the first images you want to show. If there is a series of clear-cut topics that are discussed, perhaps take one of these at a time.*

Follow the audio: *Alternatively, you may prefer to start editing all of your audio content first, so you can clearly outline your program's structure. If it is a scripted documentary, told entirely through narration, put the audio down first in order to establish your total running time.*

With an unscripted documentary comprised primarily of "talking heads," the best option may be to edit them first to see how the various interviews interconnect. With this process it's normal to end up with over two hours of footage that you then have to condense down. It does not matter what you start working on first, as long as whatever it is compels you to start editing.

In the sequence above, special effects artist Tom Sullivan talks about working on the first Evil Dead *movie.*

Tom Sullivan

1 When a new person is introduced in the documentary, it is best to show them first before you begin cutting to other footage. The "lower third" caption is used to identify the interview.

2 When the person begins talking, this is the time to switch to the B-roll footage. Generally, a dissolve (see page 113) is much smoother than a cut, particularly when it's about something that happened in the past.

3 The B-roll here is a still photo, which is shown for a total of ten seconds while the interviewee is talking about it. In this case, it is a still photo of Tom Sullivan working on "The Book of The Dead" from EVIL DEAD 1.

4 The scene then cuts back to the interviewee rather than dissolving (as in 2). It is much smoother to use a cut when you are ending an image rather than going to it.

KEY POINTS:
A methodical start

> Go through each tape (or video card), one by one.
> Divide your clips into clearly labeled bins when you are capturing your footage so that you know where everything is. For example, the interview footage of one person, with their specific B-roll, should go in one bin. Stock footage should also be divided into bins and labeled as such.
> Edit what comprises the majority of the audio first (interviews/voice-overs/narration).
> Add B-roll after you have edited your content/structure and have the final length of your program.

Lesson 32 : **Determining what is relevant**

Everything in your documentary must work toward explaining and showing what it is about. You do not want to go off on unnecessary tangents, no matter how interesting they may be.

> **Objectives**

> To ensure that what you are editing propels the story forward and is not repetitive or boring.

> To determine whether your audio and visual elements will fit together, and to ensure that they are specific to your documentary's focus.

● >>> **Assignment 32**

Watch ten minutes of a documentary. Note how the information presented moves the story along. Make a list of information that is repeated, and images that do not match the story. If the images do work, why is this?

You may find it difficult to narrow down your editing choices, especially if you have some great material that really has nothing to do with the rest of the documentary. When you are cutting your interviews and voice-overs, make sure they contribute to the telling of the main story. This will help you in your editing choices, especially if you are trying to keep the program to a specific length. If you shot over 30 hours of footage for a one-hour documentary, your first "rough" edit may be an hour and a half or two hours long. It's at this point you'll have to be more ruthless with your choices and whittle down the program to your desired length. You will end up keeping the most direct, concise information.

Repetition

Be careful not to repeat information too often. It is acceptable to do this if the documentary is an hour or an hour and a half in length, in order to remind the viewers what the issues are, but you don't want to bore or irritate them by hitting them over the head with the same points. Similarly, don't repeat any of the same visuals. Your viewer will pick up on this. For example, if you need to show someone doing an activity that's supposed to take place on different days, do not show them wearing the same clothes, since it looks as if you shot them all on the same day (which you probably did). Hopefully you will have thought of this ahead of production and shot your subjects in different changes of clothes for this precise reason. This is why "shooting for editing" is so important.

Relevant visuals

You have much more flexibility with images in your choices in B-roll, stock footage, and photos. If someone is recounting their early childhood and you do not have any photos or pictures of them at that age, it is perfectly acceptable to show close-ups of old toys or stock footage from that time period. Re-creations may also be used. Context is everything. However, you do not want to force something if it doesn't belong—for example, including a beautiful shot of waterfalls or an eagle flying that has no relevance to your story. The visuals should always complement or augment the audio.

Is the message clear?

Since you have a limited amount of time in which to present your program, it's important that both your audio and visuals are clear and to the point. Automatically eliminate bad audio (such as microphone interference) and shots that are blurry or not well composed. Utilize your best audio and visual work.

● TECHNIQUE FILE
Determining relevancy

It's important to stay focused on what your documentary is about. What is the information and overall message you want to convey? Constantly asking yourself this question will help guide you when you are making editing choices. There are four key points to remember:

1 Use only interviews and footage that move the story along.
2 Avoid repetition with audio and visuals.
3 Make sure the content is engaging.
4 Make sure the quality of your audio and visuals is good.

Levels of relevancy

Here is a three-minute segment from the documentary "I'm Not Nuts": Living with Food Allergies, which was shot on two different days. You can see from the shots shown here, there are different levels of relevancy.

Shots 1–2: *The parents of two food-allergic children discuss the difficulties in taking their allergic children out to eat at a restaurant, an activity that requires a lot of forethought, since one of their kids is allergic to wheat, and the other to dairy. Obviously, these shots convey key information and so they are entirely relevant.*

Shots 3–6: *After the interview was shot, it was noted to get additional footage of the family eating at a restaurant. The entire meal is captured, from them traveling to and entering the restaurant, to placing their orders, and enjoying their meals. Compared with shots 1–3, this footage isn't directly relevant to the message of the program—it doesn't exactly move the story along—but rather than watching the "talking heads" of the parents the entire time, this additional footage directly complements what they are talking about. The children are also very entertaining—and they are the focus—so these visuals do enrich the film, and make the story more personal.*

Shot 7: *The older sister talks about dealing with her allergies in school, for example, during an art class, where she might be allergic to some ingredients in art supplies. This is completely relevant to the program.*

Shot 8: *Since it was not possible to get footage of her in school and no photos were available, video is used of her and her sister drawing at their kitchen table. This could be considered irrelevant and discarded, but it could also be made to work. The visual is not as literal as those in the restaurant sequence but it is in effect an art class, and may be preferable to more "talking heads."*

Lesson 33 : Using transitions and special effects

No matter how cool they may be, special effects and transitions always need to have a purpose. The point of editing is not to draw attention to itself.

Someone watching a documentary should not realize it has been edited, so most of the transitions, particularly if they signify time, will be dissolves or a fade to black. The use of wipes, where the image from the next scene replaces that of the first, is also acceptable. Your editing system will undoubtedly have a wide selection of transitions to choose from; however, this does not mean you have to use *all* of them.

Transitions

Keep in mind that the transitions need to fit the picture. For example, a ripple dissolve going from one person talking to another would be jarring, and will make the first person appear to be morphing into the second. However, the same transition, this time from a person to an image of what they are talking about, may work, particularly if they are recalling something that has happened in their past.

Special effects

Think of special effects and elaborate graphics as a bonus. They are not going to make or break a documentary, unless you're making "Walking with Raptors," in which top-of-the-line computer-generated effects are needed to show what a living, extinct creature could possibly look like. Use special effects only if they add something necessary to the story. Viewers will not notice if there are few effects, but they will notice if there are far too many. Less is, most definitely, more in this instance.

**KEY POINTS:
Using transitions
and special effects**

> Transitions need to smoothly bridge between one image and the next.
> Use special effects only if they are necessary.

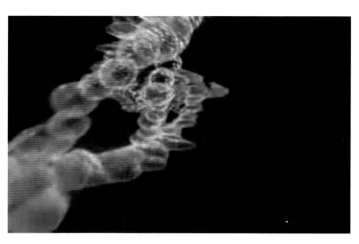

Adding production value
Tasmanian Tiger: End of Extinction *(2002) uses computer animation of a DNA strand when scientists talk about the possibility of cloning this extinct marsupial. This special effect both adds production value and provides a different shot than a B-roll of scientists looking through a microscope.*

> > > **Assignment 33** ●

List five transition effects you will need to use when editing your documentary, and also why you need them.

Basic transitions

The simpler the transitions the better, as you do not want them to stick out and detract from the content of the documentary. That said, you can get away with more creative transitions when you're using a lot of photos.

Take a look at the transitions shown and decide which might have a place in your documentary. Remember, it's vitally important that the transitions fit the tone of your program. If you have a low-key documentary about hunger in a major U.S. city, you are probably not going to want too many effect-laden transitions.

1 Cut
> One shot changes instantly to another, with no crossover.

2 Dissolve
> With this, one shot merges or fades into the next. Also called a "cross fade."

3 Page peel
> The first shot "peels" away to reveal the next. This transition gives the effect of turning a page of a book.

4 Wipe
> One video image is replaced with another image that moves across the screen. This can be as simple as going right to left, up to down, or with certain shapes, such as a circle wipe, which usually starts from the center of the screen. These transitions have a certain energy and are used for a specific purpose, such as to reveal something.

5 Dip to/from black
> The image goes quickly to a black screen, then back to an image, such as with a television commercial break or a title credit sequence.

6 Fade to/from black
> The picture appears from a black screen and vice versa.

7 Slide
> One shot "moves over" another, like one picture sliding over another.

1 Cut

2 Dissolve/cross fade

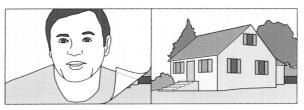

3 Page peel

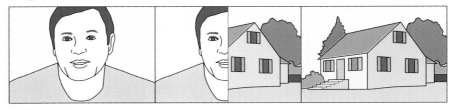

4 Wipe

5 Dip to/from black   **6 Fade to/from black**

7 Slide

Lesson 34 : Adding music and sound effects

Music and sound effects add to the production, but should not draw attention to themselves. Adding them is one of the final tasks undertaken while editing, and it is imperative that you ensure that they do not overwhelm the volume of the talking or narration.

> ## Objective
>
> > To determine what kind of music or sound effects your documentary may need, and how best to acquire them.

Music

The purpose of music is to set the mood or provoke an emotional response in a scene. Music can feature throughout the entire documentary, or just in key segments. It also connects scenes and visuals together.

Consider the type of music you might need; perhaps country or rap, rock, or elevator music. If the music is to go under the interviews, to emphasize what is being talked about, make sure you use instrumentals that do not take the viewer's attention away from the speaker. Background music with vocals is fine for the beginning and end credits, but will clash with any dialogue.

On a low-budget production, licensing popular music will be too cost-prohibitive, not to mention time-consuming when it comes to legalities and contracts. Therefore, using original music is the best option. One way to do this is to find already existing music that may fit your documentary. Place advertisements on online film production sites, stating the type of music you are looking for. Often you can find something that will fit.

Match your music
Instrumental music works best in a documentary, as it often needs to go under the sounds of someone talking, whether it be a narrator or an interviewee. Music that is sung will usually go over a title sequence, a sequence of images in which there is no talking, or during the end credits. It's of utmost importance that if a song is used, it fits the tone of the documentary.

If you have time and want the music to sync exactly with your program, another choice is to have someone create the music from scratch. Once you secure a musician, give them a copy of the edited documentary to watch. Tell the musician which sections you need music for and the type of music required, even if it is as vague as describing it as upbeat, depressed, or manic. The more specific you are, the more closely the music will match your intentions.

Another option is to buy royalty-free music. This is basically the audio version of stock footage. The benefit of going down this route is that you can listen to literally thousands of tracks online. Fees will vary greatly and there are stipulations on whether it is for "broadcast" or "non-broadcast" use. In this case it is better to be safe than sorry and purchase the broadcast contract.

Sound effects

Sound effects are often added to create ambiance in a shot or scene, such as the noise of crickets at night or the wind howling during a winter snowstorm. They can be recorded by you or taken from a sound effects library. Like music, they are added if they improve the scene. They can also replace unusable sound recorded on the original footage, such as the droning of an airplane overhead or people talking in the background. It is perfectly acceptable to add these sounds since you are maintaining the reality of the scene. The viewer will not even realize that these are not the real sounds.

Music release form
If you do choose to use original music, make sure that your musicians sign a music release form. This form gives you permission to use the music within the context of your documentary, and states that it is original and that the musicians own the copyright to it.

WHAT TO WATCH

Music is a strong point in *Koyaanisqatsi: Life Out of Balance* (1982), which has no narration or interviews. It is a series of shots that shows mankind's intrusion on Earth, and the Philip Glass score, which also serves as sound effects of a sort, conveys an uneasy feel, and a sense of dread, which is what the director intends.

In *Crumb* (1994), old 30s and 40s jazz/blues music is used over a montage of the artist, Robert Crumb's, drawings. It unites the images and is probably similar to the music he listened to when he was drawing them. The music has a personal meaning to the subject of this documentary.

Weird U.S. (2004). This television series, based on the series of bestselling books, has "Addams Family"-like music to emphasize the strangeness of the program.

● > > > Assignment 34

Go to a scene in a documentary and mute the volume. Watch it for several minutes, then write down the type of music you think best fits that scene. After you have done this, turn up the volume and listen to the music the filmmakers used. Is it similar to your choice?

MUSIC RELEASE FOR _____

I agree to let _____
use the following music I created/composed to be included in the context of the documentary _____.
The music is original and created by me.

Music:

_____

_____

_____

_____

_____

I understand that the documentary will be distributed to the home video/DVD market and any other markets including cable, pay per view, Internet, broadband, worldwide, and that the only compensation I will receive is proper credit in the documentary and 1 copy of the completed program on DVD. It is also understood that the music is copyrighted by
_____

Screen credit (as it should read)

_____

Signed and agreed (please sign and print both name and also include address, phone, and e-mail)

_____

_____

_____

Signed (producer)

_____

Producer address here:

Lesson 35 : Making arresting openers

What someone sees and hears in the first few minutes of a documentary greatly influences whether they will watch the rest of the program, so the first few minutes of your documentary need to hook the viewer's attention and lead immediately into what it is about.

> **Objectives**
> To edit an introductory scene that entices the viewer to keep watching.

Visual encouragement

The opener can be anywhere between one and five minutes, though most average at two to three minutes. It does not necessarily need to feature a lot of graphics or effects. Content is the most important thing here. Think of the opener as a tease for the program, and ascertain whether it will encourage a viewer to continue watching.

During editing, your introduction may be one of the last items you put together. By then you will be extremely familiar with the footage and have established the flow of the documentary. In fact, the tease can incorporate footage that is seen later in the documentary, as a glimpse of what is to come. This works best with a small clip from an interview, such as someone saying, "I would never have thought that it could happen to me," which is later seen in its full context. Often these first few minutes will pose a question, or introduce an investigation or a quest to solve a mystery or find an answer.

There is also the choice to simply feature the documentary's title, then go right into the documentary. Explanatory text or a quote is another option, if that works best.

Whatever you choose, most importantly the opener must fit the tone and feel of the rest of the documentary.

Visual openers
The beginning of Who Killed The Electric Car? *(2006) sets a slightly sarcastic tone for the rest of the documentary, which is primarily about how the big car companies buried this energy-saving vehicle.*

WHAT TO WATCH

Prehistoric Megastorms (2008), a History Channel miniseries consisting of six episodes—Hypercane, Volcanic Winter, Prehistoric English Superflood, Noah's Great Flood, Mega Tsunami, and Comet Storm—all of which have a similar introduction. The 1.5 minute intro states the premise of the disaster; there are lots of graphics and computer animation of the events combined with brief clips of interviews with scientists, which are then tied together with a cryptic voice-over that ends with, "And could it happen again?"

Who Killed the Electric Car? (2006)
The first few minutes of this film begin with a large outdoor funeral, which is revealed to be for an electric car. Of course, this is all staged and rather dramatic, but it effectively gets the point across and is a good example of an arresting opener. The narration, by Martin Sheen, explains that these cars were introduced in 1996, and gone within ten years.

● >>> **Assignment 35**

Based on your subject, write down several interesting ways you can begin your documentary.

KEY POINTS: Making openers

The first few minutes of a documentary should grab the viewer's interest and make them want to watch more. Here are some ideas for openers for a range of documentary subjects.

Bottled water
1 A montage of everyday people drinking all different brands of bottled water.
2 Show how water is bottled in a water bottling business.
3 Contrasting various sources of water together, such as wells, faucets, and lastly, bottled water.

Bilingual education in schools
1 An American classroom in Dearborn, Michigan, teaching English as a second language to a predominantly Middle-Eastern student body. Dearborn, Michigan, has the highest Middle-Eastern population in the country.
2 A montage of different language classes, from French to German to Spanish.
3 Focus on a teacher, talking about how language education has changed in schools this past decade.

Science-fiction conventions
1 Montage of interviews of the people who go to science-fiction conventions.
2 Showing someone getting ready in an elaborate costume and finding out it's for a science-fiction convention, where they have a contest for best costume.
3 Interviews of the guests, perhaps celebrities, who now make their living on the convention circuit (like former Star Trek actors).

Weight-gain in the Midwest
1 Montage of various shots of overweight people out in public, as a voice over explains the gist of the documentary.
2 Interview clips of various obese people talking about why they weigh so much, intercut with what they are referring to (soda pop, fast food, lack of exercise, etc.).

3 Interviews with administrator(s) in a hospital explaining how gastric bypass surgery (for obese people) is a booming business in the Midwest.

Are identical twins really similar?
1 Montage of various shots going back and forth between the everyday activities of a pair of identical adult twins, with a voice-over explaining what the documentary is about.
2 A twin talking about how he (or she) was separated from their twin as a child and how when they reunited years later found out all these similarities (or not).
3 Sets of twins being asked whether they think they are similar or not.

The fear spread by television news
1 Elderly people being asked if they are afraid of what they see on the news.
2 Clips of a newscaster giving the news, intercut with an interview of them talking about "How fear sells."
3 "Man-on-the-street" interviews of people talking about whether the news makes them afraid of things and why.

How not reproducing is the greenest thing you can do
1 Montage of people shots, perhaps with computer graphics of graphs/statistics showing how the human population has doubled in the past 40 years and what this means for our future resources.
2 Interviews with couples who have decided not two have children because of their beliefs/overpopulation.
3 A large family taking a carload of paper, plastic, and bottles to be recycled because they think they are "saving the planet."

Lesson 36 : **Title sequence and credits**

The primary function of the credits is to clearly convey
information. Anything extra is a bonus.

> "I'm Not Nuts": Living with Food Allergies
>
> TRT: 58:40
>
> Closed-captioned
>
> Produced by
> Kevin J. Lindenmuth
> Brimstone Media Productions
> phone/fax: 810 225-3079

*1 If the program is for
television, a "slate" is
required. This lists the
title, the running time,
whether it is closed-
captioned or not,
and the production
company and contact
information. It may
also specify whether the
audio is stereo or mono.*

> "I'm Not Nuts":
> Living with Food Allergies

*2 Often, a documentary
may only have the title
at the beginning and the
rest of the production
credits at the end of the
movie. This is to engage
the viewer in the
program immediately.*

> **Objective**
> > To ensure that you list everyone involved with
> the production in the end credits, in a style
> that suits the rest of the film.

Title credits

The introductory credits for a documentary may
stand alone or be incorporated into the opening
sequence. They are usually 20–60 seconds in
length and include the program's title, the
producer and director, and perhaps the composer,
if they are integral to the program. The remainder
of the credits are listed at the end. After all, you
do not want to bore your viewer before the
program even begins.

These credits can take the form of simple white
letters against a black background, or be as
complicated as computer-generated animation.
Take into consideration the size of the text, the
colors and textures used, and whether there are
layered effects. Should the credits go over a series
of clips? Should they be edited in sync with the
documentary's music? Whatever you decide,
remember that the style used should match the
tone and feel of the rest of the documentary, not
stand apart from it. Think before you create Star
Wars-style credits on your pottery documentary.

End credits

While the choices for a title sequence are limitless, end credits are much more basic. These are typically scrolling credits that list every person involved with the documentary, usually in white text against a black background. Make the letters large enough so that they can be clearly read on a television screen, since although the film might be projected on a big screen at a festival, most viewers will probably watch the DVD. These credits can also be superimposed over images if it is not too distracting; you want people to watch the credits, not what's going on behind them. Credits can also be done as separate pages, listing a few credits at a time.

PBS has a strict requirement that the end credits cannot be more than one minute in length. For a DVD release it is recommended that the end credits total no more than three minutes. Viewers appreciate a concise credit listing.

As with the title credits, end credits need to fit the rest of the documentary.

SUGGESTED ORDER FOR END CREDITS
- Title
- Executive producers
- Producer
- Director
- Editor
- Music
- Crew (camera, lighting, production assistants)
- Stock footage
- "Special thanks"
- Contact information
- Copyright information

> > > Assignment 36

Think of all the elements that will comprise your introductory credits. Are they simple or complicated?

"I'm Not Nuts": Living with Food Allergies

Shot/Edited/Directed & Produced by Kevin J. Lindenmuth

Original Music by Lindsay Martha Marie Luoma

Associate Producer Audra Hartwig

Stock footage: Elite Stock Footage

Foodallergykids.com

Cheli's Chile Restaurant
Gerry & Terri Vento

Glass Planet Industries
Stephen C. Seward

Anna Ricci Johnson
Alex Baker
Shaney Pompura
Kellen Pompura
Julie Steffes
Ian Steffes
Ariana Steffes
Marie Urban
Rose Martin
Michael Martin
Joshua Martin
McKenzie Martin

1 The end credits list everyone involved in the production, normally with the crew members first. They may also reiterate the program's title.

2 The latter part of the end credits will include acknowledgments of those who were either involved with or helped with the production. These people are listed under the "Special thanks" heading. The order in which they are listed is up to the filmmaker—they may be organized alphabetically or by importance.

PUBLICITY AND DISTRIBUTION

Publicizing your film is an important and necessary step toward distribution, so spend as much time on publicity as you have on any other aspect of the production.

Your goal in creating a "buzz" is to ensure people remember the title of your documentary and what it is about. You have worked extremely hard to complete your project, so you don't want it to end up sitting on a shelf or in a hard drive. No one cares more about the program than you, so who is more qualified to create the hype? Do everything you can think of to get the film reviewed both in print and on the Internet. Contact your local newspapers. Send out e-mail inquiries to review websites. Upload a trailer and select clips from the program to dozens of shared video sites. Submit to the film festivals. Do everything you can to get the word out that your project exists and to make people excited about it. This publicity should reach potential viewers as well as distributors, so that by the time it is available for sale they are ready to buy it.

Reviews
Keep in mind that while one reviewer will rave about your creation, another may think it's just "okay." Don't let this get you down. Remember, reviewers are individuals with different preferences. Not all of them are going to love your program. However, the good reviews will allow you to lift quotes for everything from your website to posters to the box cover art.

Distribution
In today's market many distributors expect you to do the majority of the publicity legwork. They will want to see a list of all the good review quotes and the film festivals your documentary has screened at. This enables them to better gauge whether or not they can sell and market your program. The more information they have at their disposal, the better.

Putting in the hard work publicizing your documentary increases your chances of landing a distributor and selling lots of copies. Even if you ultimately decide to self-distribute, sending out copies for review is still time well spent.

CONTENTS	PAGES

Lesson 37 : Create a trailer

One of the most important tools when marketing and publicizing your documentary is a trailer, since this will form the most widely seen element of your publicity. On the Internet, far more people will watch your trailer than read any written review, so make sure you take the time to edit together a trailer they will want to watch.

> ## Objective
> > To edit a trailer that "sells" your film, giving the viewer a reason to watch the entire documentary.

Your trailer gives the viewer their very first impression of your program, so it must pique their interest. You only get one shot. Within two and a half minutes the trailer must sum up what the film is about, show key images and clips, and give a sense of what the viewer can expect to come away with, without giving away the ending. Because your documentary is based on fact, your trailer cannot be misleading. It must represent the tone of the program and contain only footage from the film.

American Movie

American Movie chronicles the three-year journey of Wisconsin filmmaker Mark Borchardt as he makes his 16-mm short horror film *Coven* (pronounced Cove-in) with the help of friends, relatives, and actors from a local theater company. Through his interaction with these people we see his passion and quirky, good-natured personality, which is often quite hilarious. The trailer begins with stark, black-and-white shots from the movie over which we hear a blood-curdling scream. It then cuts to his best friend Mike Shank in a studio, supplying the scream. In the next few minutes we're given an overview of a variety of situations, such as casting a scene, and are introduced to contrasting personality types such as his ancient uncle (who is the producer) and actors with attitude. The trailer gives a taste of what the viewer can expect to see in the movie.

Stills from the movie, below.

KEY POINTS:
What a trailer does

> Piques the viewer's interest.
> Sums up what the film's about.
> Conveys the tone of the program.

> > > **Assignment 37**

Watch three different trailers for feature documentaries. How does each one present its beginning, middle, and end?

TECHNIQUE FILE

Editing together the best possible trailer

The best time to edit together a trailer is after you have edited the complete documentary, at which point you will be very familiar with your content and know which clips to show.

1 Take notes while watching the film: Write down which parts jump out and convey the most information in the shortest amount of time. You may find that you need to rearrange the order of interviews and footage so that the trailer flows together.

2 Sort your sound: Music and/or narration may also cover the whole length of the trailer. Sometimes the narration must be written specifically for the trailer, so that it can encapsulate what the film is about.

3 Connect with your audience: When editing the trailer, ask yourself why someone will watch your documentary to begin with, identifying your audience as you did when you first decided on your subject.

4 Work with what you've got: If you are having trouble coming up with a trailer, a good alternative may be to simply adapt the teaser you created for the opener at the very beginning, since it serves much the same purpose.

WHAT TO WATCH

Good places to watch trailers for documentaries online are:

- www.imdb.com
- www.youtube.com
- www.traileraddict.com
- www.vimeo.com
- www.moviefone.com

What the Bleep Do We Know?

What the Bleep Do We Know? (2004) tries to bridge the rift between science and spirituality and explains the New World view that people are not separate from the world or the universe. The content shows and explains how everything is connected—and that quantum physics is a part of this. It interviews the world's top physicists, biologists, engineers, and mystics, combined with animation and dramatic "reenactments" with actress Marlee Matlin, bringing all of this together into an upbeat, positive message and an intriguing look at how we influence our own reality. The two-minute trailer begins with computer animation and dramatic graphics with various voice-overs saying "It's very mysterious," "It's a question we don't have an answer to," and "The more you look at quantum physics, the more wonderful and mysterious it becomes." It then shows quick clips of the content, from nature shots to the interviews, continuing with voice-overs such as "What is reality?" and "The real trick to life is to not be in the know, it's to be in the mystery." It ends the documentary by equating the program to a "look down Alice's rabbit hole" and promises to take the viewer on an intriguing journey exploring life's mysteries.

Stills from the movie, right.

Lesson 38 : Internet publicity

You want people to access information about your documentary, and the Internet makes it very easy for them to do just that. The majority of your publicity will come through the Internet, whether it be garnering reviews or simply posting information about your film.

> ## Objective
>
> > To fully utilize the free publicity available online, and make it easy for potential viewers to find information about your documentary.

KEY POINTS:
Internet publicity

> Create an informational website about the documentary.
> Post your trailer on numerous shared video sites.
> Contact online movie review sites.
> Reach out to filmmaking sites.

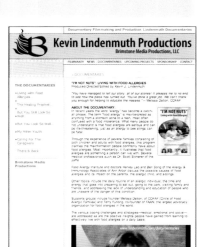

Your film's website

A good way to begin your marketing is to create a website specifically for your production. This will include information both for the casual viewer as well as the press. It may even attract the attention of a distributor.

The website should feature a synopsis of what the documentary is about, a listing of the cast and crew credits, along with short biographies and plenty of photos from the production. If you did not take any photographs you can lift frame-grabs from the digital video. Don't forget to include the trailer and to list your contact information. When you begin getting reviews and festival showings, post these on the website as well. In fact, you could create the website as soon as you decide on your title and, once production begins, keep a daily blog or video diary to update people on your progress.

Other websites

Once your website is up and running, look for others that are friendly to independent productions. Offer information about your documentary to blogs and review sites, no matter how small. Direct them to your website so they can see if your program is something they might like to review. Remember, your independent

Go public

The website here provides all the information on the documentary on one page, including the synopsis, the DVD box art, and a three-minute video clip of the 85-minute program.

production is probably not going to be screened by the mainstream review sites, at least not at first. The key is to create such an Internet presence that your audience will be interested by the time you contact them.

Next, look for other websites that may be interested in reviewing and spreading the word about your documentary. If your piece is about the epidemic of diabetes in the United States, for example, contact diabetes support groups. If you have original music created for the documentary and your musician has numerous contacts at music sites, then contact all of those. They may be interested in doing an article on your documentary from that perspective.

Post your trailer on as many shared video sites as possible, with links directing viewers back to your website. Share production photos on other filmmaking sites. Inundate the Web with information about your production. The wider the net you cast, the more successful your publicity will be.

>>> **Assignment 38**

List what you think will be the five best places on the Internet to post information about your program. What are the benefits of each?

TECHNIQUE FILE

Create a press-release e-mail

Create a monthly press release that lists everything that is happening with your documentary, and e-mail it to websites and individuals who will be able to help with your publicity. Remember, raising awareness is the aim; you need to make your program's existence known to as many people as possible.

1 Provide as much information as you can
In addition to a summary of the film's content—the synopsis—include other key information such as where the film will be broadcast or where it is available, and any favorable reviews already received.

2 Add some design flair
Try to make your e-mail as visually attractive as you can. Break the content down into digestible parts, and use bold subheads to draw the reader in to the information.

3 Start with this template
Right is an example of a press-release e-mail for the documentary "I'm Not Nuts": Living with Food Allergies. *This widespread release was e-mailed to food allergy awareness groups and organizations that were considered interested parties. You might like to use this as a template for your own press-release e-mail.*

○ ○ ○   New Message

Send   Chat   Attach   Address   Fonts   Colors   Save As Draft   Photo Brow

To:
Cc:
Subject:
From: Signature: None

Hello, My name is Kevin Lindenmuth, producer of the new food-allergy documentary, *"I'm Not Nuts": Living with Food Allergies.* To view the first five minutes, go to YouTube (include link to site).

PBS broadcasts: The program is being offered to PBS through NETA (National Educational Telecommunications Association) this month (include date). Food Allergy Awareness week is May 10–16th 2009, so many other stations will be broadcasting it during this time also. The stations have permission to show the program during the next five years.

NETA programming information: See http://www.netaonline.org/search/ProgramDetails.cfm?ID=2620 This is the TV version; running time is 58 minutes.

The DVD version: The full-length version (running time 84 minutes) is available on DVD at Amazon.com (include link to the DVD).

Your library If your local library is interested in purchasing a DVD, they can order it from The Library Video Company (include link to site).

About the documentary:

[Include a synopsis here—300–500 words]
[Include your website too]

Reviews/quotes to date:
"An essential food-allergy documentary"—Sarah Hatfield, No Whey, Mama

"A must-see DVD"—Vermont Food Allergy Organization

"Am I allowed to make this required viewing for every childcare worker and educator in the country? Because I'd like to. This film clearly and carefully lays out the basics of what it's like to be food allergic and/or to have a food-allergic child."—GoDairyFree.com

"... a useful guide to food allergy for the newly diagnosed, and includes medical commentary from some well-respected names in food allergy research."—Peanut Allergy UK

"... gives great information from the medical perspective including interviews with several well-known allergists."—Allergicchild.com

"The film clarifies the misinformation people commonly have about food allergies and illustrates that food allergies are something a person can live with."—Allergen Bureau

"A fine initiation to the world of food allergies, *"I'm Not Nuts"* will be welcome in public library collections and academic health sciences collections at the senior high through junior college level, as well as those with consumer health collections."—Educational Media Reviews online

"I wish this documentary had been available when we first received the peanut allergy diagnosis! It gives all the basics in an accurate, reasonable, and reassuring way."—foodallergybuzz.com

"Yes! The food allergy documentary we've been waiting for. I feel like purchasing this for the school, family, everyone we know!"—The Nut-free Mom blogspot

Lesson 39 : Screeners and press kits

Screeners and press kits are the tools that help you
get the word out to reviewers and distributors.

Objective

> To create a screen and
press kit that reviewers
will want to watch
immediately.

KEY POINTS:
The success of
screeners and
press kits

> Offer both DVD and
downloadable screeners
to suit all.
> Make sure all DVDs that
are mailed will play.
> Adapt the press kit
depending on who it is for:
reviewer or distributor.
> Create an electronic press
kit on your website.

The screener

The DVD of the documentary you send out for
review is referred to as a "screener." On the face
label of the DVD will be printed the
documentary's title, the total running time, and
your contact information. At this point you may
even choose to create the box artwork to make it
look more enticing: this may make the difference
between someone watching it immediately or a
month after they receive it.

Before you send out a DVD, play it in your own
DVD player to make sure it works. You do not
want to be waiting months for a review, only to
find out that they received a blank disk.

Downloadable screener

An alternative to mailing out DVDs is to make
available a downloadable screener. There are
numerous sites that make this possible for a
small fee, for example, YouSendit.com. You upload
the file to their site and are sent a link to access
it. Send this link to your reviewers or potential
distributors and they can download your
documentary from the site directly to their
computer. It's often available for seven days. In
this case, your website could serve the same
purpose as a printed press kit. To help save the
expense on printing, DVD duplication, and
postage you can offer this downloadable version
first, and only mail out press kits to those who
desire a hard copy.

For your eyes only
*Often the words "for review purposes only" will be
superimposed over the bottom third of the screen: you
may be mailing out hundreds of disks and this deters
unauthorized copying.*

> > > **Assignment 39**   ●

**Make a list of the top ten
places you will mail your
first screeners to.**

Tailoring to the recipient

There are two distinct groups you will be sending screeners to: the press, which includes websites and magazines, and potential distributors. If the DVD is sent out for review, do not include the other press you have received; this will only irritate the reviewer, who may think you are telling him or her what to think. When you send a screener and press kit to a potential distributor, make sure you do include your favorable press reviews and quotes.

Most review sites and print magazines list their mailing address to send review material to. The same goes for distribution companies. However, it is always best to get a contact name, so that when you check up there's an actual person to communicate with. When you mail them a copy, make sure you get a delivery tracking number so you can make sure they did receive it. Don't be alarmed, however, if it takes several months to get a response.

The press kit

The screener DVD is often accompanied by a "press kit," a printed document that contains all the information you may already have on your website, including the synopsis of the program, the producer/director's biographies, and any other key information that makes the program stand out. It may also include interesting anecdotes about the production.

The Electronic Press Kit (EPK)

Rather than sending out printed materials, you can also send all the above information on a CD along with your DVD. You can also include photos from the production on the EPK as well.

● TECHNIQUE FILE

Creating your press kit

If you are sending your documentary out to review, you'll need to put together a comprehensive press kit. Here's what you should include:

1 Pocket folder: To file everything neatly.
2 Brief letter on company letterhead: This should introduce yourself (and/or your company) and the program. Include biographical information about the filmmaker/qualifications (and include website information).
3 A synopsis of a program: This should read like the back of a DVD cover.
4 Any interesting information: Include any extra information about the program that you think will help to "sell" it.

5 Photos from the production: These can also be sent on a CD.
6 DVD of the program: Send this along with box artwork.
7 Favorable review quotes: To help sell the program. Only include review quotes if the press kit is for a distributor; if it's for a reviewer, do not include previous reviews. You do not want to be seen to influence them.

Appearance is everything
You should endeavor to make your press kit as aesthetically pleasing as possible. Make it colorful, include graphics, and break content down into digestible sections. Remember: this is essentially a sales tool for your documentary; you need to sell it!

Lesson 40 : Film festivals

Showing your film at festivals is a way to get recognition and publicity, and could directly land you a distribution deal.

KEY POINTS: Choosing festivals

> Is entering a festival the right thing to do with your particular program?
> Determine your budget for entry fees. How many festivals can you enter?
> Which festivals are the best to enter?
> Is the festival to get distribution or publicity?

● >>> **Assignment 40**

Pick five film festivals that are most suited to your documentary. How much will it cost for you to enter all five? If the cost is prohibitive, how can you narrow down your choice?

Distribution companies, both DVD and theatrical, regularly send representatives to the more prominent film festivals, so those are the ones to target if you are interested in getting this type of attention.

If you made the documentary with the intention of getting it on television and have obtained underwriters, there is little reason to enter it into a film festival other than to have it shown to an audience and perhaps get some recognition.

Which festivals?

Worldwide, there are hundreds of film festivals that accept documentaries. At no other time in history have they been so popular. It is simply a matter of choosing the festivals your documentary will fit the best.

Keep in mind that the majority of film festivals are not free, which could result in a fair amount of expense if you plan on entering numerous festivals. There is also the time factor and the obligatory waiting if the festival is six months down the line. The majority of festivals also want your program "new," so it cannot yet be broadcast or distributed.

Just because you submitted to a festival does not mean they are going to choose to show it.

Wide-ranging appeal

It's often a thrill to get accepted in a foreign film festival. However, make sure that your documentary has "universal appeal." If it's about a very specific subject intended for a specific audience, then it may not be accessible to a different crowd.

Your documentary may be competing against thousands of others. It also has to appeal to the festival judges, who have their specific likes, dislikes, and opinions. On the other hand, if your documentary does get accepted and is a winner, this can quickly open doors to more distribution and publicity than all of your previous efforts. Even if it did not win first place, putting "Official Selection" on your publicity material is still impressive.

DOCU MENT ARY edGe FESTIVAL

2010

AUCKLAND
RIALTO CINEMAS NEWMARKET
27th FEB – 14th MARCH
WELLINGTON
ANGELIKA AT READING CINEMAS COURTENAY
13th MARCH – 28th MARCH

www.documentaryedge.org.nz

● TECHNIQUE FILE

Hold your own screening

While you are waiting for reviews of all the screeners you sent out, hold a screening of your film at a local venue, such as a bar, library, or theater—most theaters are equipped with digital projectors that you can hook a DVD player up to. This event will get you in the local newspapers and help spread good reviews by word of mouth. Also, this screening could serve as a gesture toward everyone involved with helping on the project, from the crew to the people you interviewed. They will enjoy seeing the program on a big screen, and it validates their involvement with the project. You could also sell copies of the DVD and immediately recoup some income.

music of the 1960s that defined a generation. 90 min.

THE MAKE-BELIEVERS *World Premiere*

Wednesday, July 22 at 7:30pm $9 Members / $12 Public / Incl. Rece
In Person: Huntington Filmmaker Glenn Andreiev
Who looks at your private life as it zips through cyber-space? The M
Believers examines these questions in informative and humorous w
Among the people interviewed are Wiliam Sherman, a Daily New
Reporter who used his computer to steal the Empire State Building, a
homeless gambling addict who scammed over six figures with a laptop,
Huntington-based filmmaker Glenn Andreiev has made a number of
films, including Silver Night, and The Deed To Hell. 2009, USA, 80 min

UNRAVELLING MICHELLE

Film festivals that accept documentaries

1 **ATLANTA INTERNATIONAL DOCUMENTARY FILM FESTIVAL:** www.docufest.com/home.html
2 **AMNESTY FILM FESTIVAL:** www.amnestyfilmfestival.nl
3 **BERLIN INTERNATIONAL FILM FESTIVAL:** www.berlinale.de
4 **BIG SKY FILM FESTIVAL:** www.bigskyfilmfest.org
5 **BIG SKY DOCUMENTARY FILM FESTIVAL:** http://bigsky.bside.com
6 **BROOKLYN INTERNATIONAL FILM FESTIVAL:** www.wbff.org
7 **CALIFORNIA INTERNATIONAL DOCUMENTARY FILM FESTIVAL:** www.sjiff.org/caldocfest/index.html
8 **CAMDEN INTERNATIONAL FILM FESTIVAL:** www.camdenfilmfest.org
9 **CANNES FILM FESTIVAL:** www.festival-cannes.com
10 **CHICAGO INTERNATIONAL DOCUMENTARY FESTIVAL:** www.chicagodocfestival.org
11 **DOCFEST:** www.docfest.org
12 **DOCNZ DOCUMENTARY FILM FESTIVAL:** www.docnz.org.nz
13 **DOXA DOCUMENTARY FILM FESTIVAL:** www.doxafestival.ca
14 **EAST SILVER DOCUMENTARY FILM MARKET:** www.nomadsland.com/events/east-silver-documentary-film
15 **ENVIRONMENTAL FILM FESTIVAL:** www.dcenvironmentalfilmfest.org
16 **FAIRFAX DOCUMENTARY FILM FESTIVAL:** www.fairfaxdocfest.org

17 **FULL FRAME DOCUMENTARY FILM FESTIVAL:** www.fullframefest.org
18 **GI FILM FESTIVAL:** www.gifilmfestival.com
19 **GLOBIANS DOCFEST BERLIN:** www.globians.com
20 **HOLLYWOOD DOCUMENTARY FILM FESTIVAL:** http://hollywoodawards.com/docs
21 **HOT DOCS CANADIAN INTERNATIONAL DOCUMENTARY FESTIVAL:** www.hotdocs.ca
22 **HOT SPRINGS DOCUMENTARY FILM FESTIVAL:** http://www.hsdff.org
23 **IFI STRANGER THAN FICTION DOCUMENTARY FILM FESTIVAL:** www.irishfilm.ie
24 **INTERNATIONAL DOCUMENTARY FILM FESTIVAL AMSTERDAM:** www.german-films.de/app/festival-guides/festival
25 **IOWA CITY DOCUMENTARY FILM FESTIVAL:** www.icdocs.net
26 **LOS ANGELES FILM FESTIVAL:** http://www.lafilmfest.com
27 **NASHVILLE FILM FESTIVAL:** www.nashvillefilmfestival.org
28 **NEWPORT BEACH FILM FESTIVAL:** www.newportbeachfilmfest.com
29 **NEWPORT INTERNATIONAL FILM FESTIVAL:** www.newportfilmfestival.com
30 **NEW YORK FILM FESTIVAL:** www.filmlinc.com/nyff
31 **OXDOX INTERNATIONAL FILM FESTIVAL:** www.oxdox.com
32 **PORTLAND DOCUMENTARY AND EXPERIMENTAL FILM FESTIVAL:** www.pdxfilmfest.com

33 **ROVING EYE DOCUMENTARY FESTIVAL:** www.film-festival.org/RovingEye.php
34 **SEBASTOPOL DOCUMENTARY FILM FESTIVAL:** http://www.sebastopolfilmfestival.org
35 **SHEFFIELD INTERNATIONAL FILM FESTIVAL:** https://sheffdocfest.com
36 **SILVERDOCS:** www.silverdocs.com
37 **SLAMDANCE:** www.slamdance.com
38 **SUNDANCE FILM FESTIVAL:** http://festival.sundance.org/2010/
39 **SXSW FILM FESTIVAL:** http://sxsw.com/film
40 **SYDNEY FILM FESTIVAL:** www.sydneyfilmfestival.org
41 **TEXAS INTERNATIONAL DOCUMENTARY FILM FESTIVAL:** www.thinlinefilmfest.com
41 **THESSALONIKI INTERNATIONAL FILM FESTIVAL:** www.filmfestival.gr
42 **TORONTO INTERNATIONAL FILM FESTIVAL:** www.tiff.net/default.aspx
43 **TRIBECA FILM FESTIVAL:** http://www.tribecafilm.com/festival
44 **UNITED NATIONS ASSOCIATION FILM FESTIVAL:** www.unaff.org
45 **VAIL FILM FESTIVAL:** www.vailfilmfestival.org
46 **WISCONSIN FILM FESTIVAL:** http://http://wifilmfest.org
47 **YAMAGATA INTERNATIONAL DOCUMENTARY FILM FESTIVAL:** www.yidff.jp/home-e.html

Lesson 41 : Television

Although the country in which you reside may have certain requirements and stipulations in regard to broadcasting independent productions, the good thing is that you can submit your program to the worldwide television market.

Objective

> Send your screener to the appropriate television channel.

● >>> Assignment 41

Looking at the program packaging requirements on page 131, write down the information that is going to be included on your visual slate.

Approaching channels

Before you send a screener to a specific television channel, make sure it fits their guidelines. If you made a documentary on the North American honeybee massacre of 1988 and expect Animal Planet or the Discovery Channel to eagerly pick it up, you will likely be disappointed. Many television channels, such as National Geographic and A&E, produce their own documentaries and rarely take any independent product. Their policies will be listed on their websites. PBS frequently broadcasts independent productions, although there are several different ways to approach this market. One is to get the film accepted on a show such as Frontline or American Experience. Another is to go through a company that is a supplier of programming to PBS. These are predominantly education-oriented programs. New television channels are emerging exclusively on the Internet, and they are eager to find new programming.

Specific information

The screener and press kit you send to a television distributor will be slightly different from what you send to a DVD distributor. Clearly state whether the film is a single program or part of a series, what format it was shot in (standard definition or high definition), the length, and whether it has been broadcast before. You should also specify the audience and the demographic you intend to reach and include a list of funders, companies, and individuals who may have financed the production.

Broadcast License Agreement

If a television station does want to broadcast your program they will send you a Broadcast License Agreement to sign. It will include how much they are paying to air the program and then go into the specifics of when the station can show it and for how long. It states that you (the producer) own all the rights and have all the releases/clearances. It also lists the format and materials that you will supply them with, such as a Betacam SP or a DVCAM tape. If you do not send them what they need and this broadcast master does not meet their technical specifications, they can reject showing the program and void the contract.

Tip

Get a name

Ring and talk to the receptionist at your chosen television company and find out who the right person to submit to is. If you just address it to the station/production company, it will get "lost in the pile." Also, getting the name of a contact will enable you to follow up after you send your screener.

PBS PROGRAM PACKAGING REQUIREMENTS

- Fifteen seconds to one minute of continuous leader at the beginning of the tape, synchronous black.
- One minute of reference signal bars and tone. This test signal is a true indication of the program's color, video, pedestal, and phase.
- A 10- to 15-second visual slate that includes the program's title, production company, length of the program, and indication of mono or stereo audio and closed captioning.
- A 10-second countdown, with 1.8 seconds of black between the end of the countdown and beginning of the program.
- The entire length of the program.
- Two minutes of black after the end of the program.

VIDEO SPECIFICATIONS

- Reference color bars shall be a true indication of the program's chroma, video, pedestal, and phase.
- Peak chrominance will not exceed 110 IRE units above the blanking level.
- Video levels shall average 100 IRE and pedestal 7.5 IRE when the VTR is in unity.
- Video, chroma, and pedestal levels shall be consistent throughout.
- Horizontal and vertical blanking shall conform to ANSI/SMPTE standards: 10.7 s, +0.3,-0.2s, and 20 lines, respectively.

AUDIO SPECIFICATIONS

- Reference tone shall be a true indication of the program's audio levels.
- Tone shall be at 0vu when the VTR is in unity.
- Audio levels shall be consistent throughout the entire program.

CLOSED CAPTIONING

- Closed captioning is required for television, which is an additional expense. There are companies that specialize in this and it can run anywhere from $300 to $1,200, depending on the length of the program and how quickly you need it finished. Whether or not this is your responsibility depends upon the television channel.

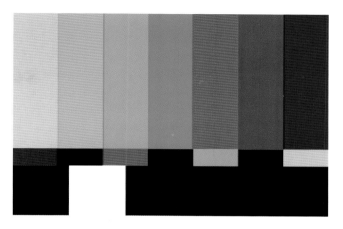

SMPTE color bars
These bars are a test pattern used to set television monitors/receivers to reproduce the chrominance and luminance information of the program correctly. These color bars can be produced with your editing software.

"I'm Not Nuts": Living with Food Allergies

TRT: 58: 40

Closed-captioned

Produced by
Kevin Lindenmuth
Brimstone Media Productions
Phone/fax: 810-225-3079

The "slate"
This identifies the program, its running time, and production company. It follows the one minute of color bars and lasts 10 seconds.

Countdown
The countdown on your broadcast tape comes after the one minute of color bars and the slate, and begins at 8 or 10 seconds, which gives the broadcaster enough time to cue the program.

Lesson 42 : **DVD sales**

The success of your documentary may hinge on DVD sales, so be well informed when deciding on your distribution method.

> **Objective**
> To decide which type of DVD distribution you are most comfortable with. This primarily depends on time and cost.

KEY POINTS: Distribution types

> Self-distribution.
> Sub-distributor.
> Exclusive distributor.
> Non-exclusive distributors via the Internet.

● >>> Assignment 42

List the pros and cons of self-distribution vs. signing with an exclusive distributor.

There are two ways in which to distribute your film on DVD. One is to license it to a distributor who has an exclusive contract with you. The other is to distribute it yourself and sell directly to the public and to sub-distributors.

Distributor

A distributor will want an exclusive agreement for a specific territory, such as North America, for a specific amount of time, usually five to seven years. If they sell overseas they may want worldwide rights. This enables them to sell your program to other distributors who sell to their specific countries.

The majority of documentary distributors market to individuals and libraries. They have hundreds, if not thousands, of titles in their catalogs. For this reason it's important to investigate them and their capabilities of getting your documentary out for sale. Can the distributor sell thousands of copies, or do they simply need another title to list in their brochure?

Investigate the distributor to make sure they are legitimate, for example by asking for references from other producers they have worked with. If they are trustworthy they will readily comply. If they only pay you a percentage and residuals on the sales, you will most likely never see any income. Take care when reading the distribution agreement. They may want to subtract their costs of advertising and other expenses out of the profit. This is why it is much better to get an up-front flat fee rather than the promise of a percentage.

As with the television channels, a DVD distributor will make a master of the program from you. This will be either on DVCPRO or DVCAM. However, they may want a digital file instead, particularly if it is shot on HD. They may also want supplemental material for the extras, such as interviews with the producer and director. Once they receive all of the material from you, they will create the artwork and market the program. At this point your work is done.

Self-distribution

With self-distribution you are responsible for the expense of duplication, boxes and packaging, and advertising. The advantage of this is that you will know exactly where every DVD is sold.

Naturally, the starting point for your sales is to offer it on your documentary website. If you publicize your documentary well, then you may immediately begin getting orders. A good portion of your sales can come from sub-distributors, who will buy copies from you for wholesale (50 to 60 percent less) and then re-sell them to their clients. Many of these sub-distributors have long-established connections with libraries and media stores and can immediately move quantities of your title.

SALES AGENTS

- *A sales agent will represent your program at the various film markets.*
- *These agents already have relationships with different types of distributors and are well worth the 15 to 25 percent they will take after they make a sale.*
- *They also know how to read contracts and therefore, it is in their best interest to get the best deal.*

Lesson 43 : **New media**

Recent advancements have created new forms of distribution on the Internet that are on a par with the quality of television and DVD. In fact, this route bypasses movie theaters, television networks, and home video altogether.

Rentals and downloads

A program is made available on the Internet either as a rental or as a download. For someone to watch or purchase your program, their computer must meet certain technical requirements, all of which are becoming standard. If it is a rental, a viewer watches it streamed, real-time, from a website. Many online DVD rental companies now offer this service on their websites and include it as part of their monthly fee.

Feature-length documentaries take about one hour to download with a fast connection. Progressive downloads enable you to start watching the film almost immediately. It is also possible to watch these videos on your regular television as long as you can hook it up to your computer. Whether or not you can burn these purchased movies to a disk depends on the licensing agreement that the online distribution company has with those particular movies—they often use security protection that prevents copying.

The paying online venues require that your documentary be supplied in digital format.

Different companies vary in their fulfillment requirements, so while one company will take a DVD and another a compressed file, others will have very specific and mandatory instructions that can be cost-prohibitive to the low-budget producer.

Non-exclusivity

The best thing about this form of distribution is that it is non-exclusive, so you can have your film available from a dozen different companies. Theoretically, the more places that offer your program, the more accessible your documentary will be to a worldwide audience. This, in turn, means more residuals for you. However, it is too early to tell if the income is comparable with the older, physical distribution methods.

PIRACY

- *Since your program is available in digital format, it makes it easier to make copies.*
- *If you find out that someone has copied your program and posted it on a site such as YouTube without permission, you can directly contact that website and tell them to remove it. The same applies to individuals selling unauthorized copies of your DVD on sites such as eBay. Remember, if someone is intent on making a copy of your program, they'll find a way to do it. The most important deterrent is to be vigilant and control the ways in which your documentary is available to the public.*

Case study: *Post-production*

With the filming of the interviews now complete, it's time to
return to the editing suite to structure the documentary, flesh out
the footage, and refine the film. Following is Kevin J. Lindenmuth's
account of the post-production process.

Editing

After filming was complete, I spent the
next month transferring each of the
MiniDV tapes to DVD. This prevents the
loss of valuable footage in the event
that fragile tapes becoming damaged. I
then begin transcribing the interviews.
When searching for specific content, it
is much more time efficient to read
through the transcripts than scan
through the original video footage.
Everything that the interviewees
say is keyed, and the time code is
written down every quarter-
page for easy reference. The
usable sections are
highlighted with a yellow
marker, as is anything
particularly emotional. It
was noted that some of
the individuals answered
the questions better than
others; a note was made of

*Part of a sample page from
an interview transcript*

*It's much quicker to skim-read a
transcript, highlighting with a marker
pen the sections you want to keep. This
transcript shows just one of the
interviewee's responses to some of the
author's questions.*

4:45
WHAT DO YOU WANT TO DO BEFORE YOU DIE?
I wake up each morning wanting to help the next person I meet. I'm
editor of a website about spiritual issues, so when I come downstairs in
the morning, in my inbox, and I take the time to answer that mail. A
good day for me is when I've interacted with someone and helped
them. I just want to keep helping people.

5:48
I'd like to see what Mt. Everest looks like, India...
Fundamentally, if my life ended tomorrow I wouldn't have any regrets
that there's anything left undone.

6:45
WHAT HAPPENS AFTER?
Do I have fears about death? In the sense of I would not like to be a
huge burden on people for a long period of time before I die,
particularly. I'd find it unpleasant to go through severe Alzheimer's
where I'm a burden on people and I don't have my personality left... For
me, living is connection with other people. That's what life is about. But
I don't fear dying.

WHAT DO YOU THINK HAPPENS AFTER?
What happens after? I don't know. I'd like to think that there is some
enduring life or connection. I like to think that our personality continues,
where we are known and know other people. I work with students, and
talked to a student what she hopes for in death... and she said, when I
die I want to continue to watch how life comes out for the other people
around me. That would be pretty powerful. There's a sense that you
want to see life continue, partly for you but people you live and
awareness after you die that that's gonna happen... and be a part of
that. (goes with Sasha and what Keith says about continuation)

8:55
I've been in several, as a journalist traveling, several near-fatal car
accidents and know from experience you go through this huge

these responses. Once this was done, all of the highlighted sections were "captured" by the editing system, in order of the transcripts and time code. The documentary would be edited within a four-month period.

Gathering B-roll

After analyzing the transcripts, the interviewees were contacted and asked to send appropriate photos. If one person was talking about the death of their brother or sister, photos of those individuals were requested. When a horror filmmaker was talking about how he treats death in a film versus his reaction to death in reality, clips from his or her films could be used.

Structuring the documentary

The program would be feature length, 80–85 minutes in total. The structure would primarily follow the order of the questions that the interviewees answered, since there was no written script. Because each question was so different from the previous and there may be no way to smoothly bridge from one question/answer to the next, there would be set chapter markers that state each question. These chapter markers would take on the simple form of white letters on a black background. The very first chapter would be the immediate attention-grabber, "How do you want to die?" The closing chapter of the documentary is "How do you want to be remembered?" and aims to leave a lasting impression with the viewers.

Special effects/transitions:

There would be no special effects, other than if they were already included in a film clip. The graphics would be simple, as would the transitions, which will include dissolves, fades, or cuts (see page 113).

Music

As with all my previous documentaries, the music would be low-key, and used to augment what the individuals were talking about. Preexisting instrumental music already had been solicited from a band, Seasons of the Wolf, who had provided music for several of my narrative features in the past.

Box artwork

Before the documentary was edited and the synopsis finalized, an artist was hired to paint the cover for the DVD box. The cover is representative of what the program is about: a human skull, which represents death, superimposed over the planet Earth. The front of the box was designed so that when the film was edited and publicity had begun, the image could be used with a range of marketing tools.

Publicity

Although *The Life of Death* documentary was intended for a widespread audience, it was also targeted at people who are followers of the interviewees. For David Crumm, this would mean those who read his spiritual column; for Art Regner, it was the Michigan sports fan, etc. These were people who may not normally watch documentaries but may do so in order to see what these individuals have to say about the subject. The interviewees would also help publicize the project when it is finished, so there would be a great deal of cross-pollination.

The majority of the publicity would be via the Internet, through specific review sites (both documentary and genre), as well as posting clips on YouTube and Facebook, for example. Local newspapers and magazines would also be contacted.

The goal for your DVD box art is to not only be representative of your program but entice people to pick it up and see what it's about.

> **TIP**
> ## Use the best photos
> *Inform your talent/interviewees what you need well beforehand, usually after you log/transcribe their interviews. This could be childhood photos, for when an artist talks about a pivotal event that affected his life, or professional publicity stills for when an actress is talking about working on a well-known movie.*

Glossary

"Action": The word you say to indicate you have begun shooting a scene.

ADR (automatic dialogue replacement): Re-recording dialogue in a studio to match what is on screen. In documentaries it is used to improve sound quality if the on-location sound is not usable, either from extraneous sounds at the location or faulty microphones.

After Effects: Digital motion graphics and compositing software by Adobe Systems used for film and video post-production.

Alpha mask/channel: Provides transparency around an object on a digital image. It is particularly used for graphics.

Ambient sound: Background noise recorded to add atmosphere to a soundtrack. Also known as "atmos" and "wildtrack." With documentaries, often recorded with "B-roll" footage.

Animation: Created from a sequence of individual images that are either drawn, modeled, or created on a computer.

Auteur: A somewhat pretentious name given to certain filmmakers and directors; often used disparagingly.

Audio clips: Individual sound items you edit with, such as a sound effect or person's sound bite.

Audio files: The source media files that the audio clips reference, such as an entire piece of music or an entire interview section.

Audio track: The timeline tracks that hold audio clips.

Aspect Ratio: Ratio of the width of the image to its height. The 4:3 aspect ratio is the "square" dimension of an old-fashioned TV set, used on many standard definition cameras. The 16:9 radio is wide-screen, used with both HD and standard cameras.

Avid Media Composer: Non-linear digital editing system created by Avid Technology Inc. that is used in the television, movie, and video industries to create TV shows, feature films, and commercials.

Bars and Tone: Video and audio test pattern standard that ensures acceptable recording levels.

B-Roll Footage: Secondary footage that is shot and adds meaning to an edited video sequence. The term can also include still photos that are used for this purpose.

Bin: The location to store media that is used in a production.

Boom: How audio may be captured during a production via a directional microphone that is attached to one end of a "fish pole," a piece of equipment that can be kept out of the camera shot.

CCD (charge couple device): This converts light into an image in a DV camera. The best cameras have three CCDs, one to handle each primary color (red, green, blue).

Camera tape: White tape, similar to duct tape, that can be written on.

Capture card: Various video capture devices that store information directly on a hard drive rather than on digital tapes.

Capturing video: Process of loading and storing video into your non-linear editing system.

Chroma key: Replacing a large area of flat color (usually blue or green) with another image such as placing a new background behind a person sitting in a studio. This is also referred to as blue screen or green screen.

Cinematography: Art of using lights and cameras to capture an image for motion pictures and video.

CGI (computer-generated imagery): Any images created by a computer, usually for special effects and animation.

Clone: Identical copy of a digital tape, as digital format does not degrade in quality.

Closed-captioning Systems developed that display text on a television or video screen, usually transcribing the audio of the program as it unfolds.

Color correction: Balancing color, often to fix or improve the continuity between different shooting times in which the lighting has changed, such as shooting during the day if sunlight is sporadic. Also used for adding color effects to film or video for effect such as giving a flashback a "sepia" tone to make it look old.

COMPOSITING: Combining two or more image elements into a single final image.

CONTINUITY: Making sure that everything on-screen looks the same, or is in order, from take to take. Certain objects, such as the time on clocks in the background, stand out if not consistent.

COPYRIGHT: An artist's legal right to control the use and reproduction of his or her work. For a program to be officially copyrighted in the US it must be registered with the Copyright Office at the Library of Congress.

CUT: The transition from one shot to another.

CRANE: Production equipment with a long jib that allows the camera to be moved to a greater height in a smooth motion.

CREDITS: List of who did what on a movie.

DIALOGUE: The spoken words.

DIGIBETA: Short for Digi-Betacam, a proprietary high-resolution video format developed by Sony.

DIGITAL ZOOM: Enlarges an image to make it appear as though a long lens was used. Causes degradation of the picture, though this can be used for an effect.

DISTRIBUTION: Getting your movie shown in as many venues as possible, which includes theaters, broadcasts, DVD, and internet streaming and downloads.

DOCUMENTARY: A factual film on any topic that is not a work of fiction.

DOLLY: A camera support with wheels that gives a smooth camera movement. It may be self-contained, like a "doorway dolly," or mounted on tracks, like a train car.

DUBBING: Replacing one language dialogue with another language. Copying from one tape to another.

DV (DIGITAL VIDEO): Any system that records moving images as digital information (ones and zeroes). Does not lose quality when copied. Popular current formats include MiniDV, HDV, DVCAM, DVCPRO, and Digi-Betacam.

EDITING: Putting all the different shots and elements of the documentary together to tell a story.

EDL: Edit decision list.

FEATURE: A movie or documentary that is usually anywhere from 70 to 200-plus minutes in length. Also referred to as feature-length.

FILTER: A piece of either glass or gelatin that goes over the camera lens and changes the color and/or the amount of light reaching the tape, such as on a very bright day. Editing software filters serve a similar function but you manipulate the footage after shooting. Filters can also be thought of as special effects.

FINAL CUT PRO: A non-linear digital editing system created by Apple that is used in the television, movie, and video industries to create TV shows, feature films, and commercials.

FIREWIRE: Apple's trademark for the IEEE 1394 interface, a serial bus standard for high-speed digital video and audio transfers. This is the cable you use when transferring footage from your camera or deck to your computer editing system.

FOCUS: Manually or automatically adjusting the elements in a lens so that an image is sharp, or not, depending on what is needed.

FOLEY SOUND: Sound effects recorded in a studio, such as footsteps or a door creaking. However, it can also include natural sounds, such as a specific bird chirp or the sound of running water. It is sound that is created/recorded to give audio to a video sequence.

FPS (FRAMES PER SECOND) The number of images captured every second on film or video. The standard for film is 24 fps; for NTSC video (North America) it is 30 (29.97) fps. Many video cameras now have the option of shooting at 24 fps.

GAIN: Amplifies the signal of the camera's image sensor which turns the brightness level up or down. The more you increase the gain the "noisier" the image gets.

GAFFER TAPE: Black cloth tape, similar to duct tape but not as sticky. It is indispensable on a film set, for everything from taping down cables to holding up reflectors, and everything in between.

GUERRILLA FILMMAKING: Usually refers to making films without getting authorized permission to use locations. It is often synonymous with independent productions.

HANDHELD: The style of shooting without using a tripod, often intentionally shaky, as if from the point of view of the observer.

HDV (HIGH-DEFINITION VIDEO): The latest video format that gives extremely high-resolution images in a 16:9 (wide-screen) format. It is quickly becoming the standard.

LAVALIER: A small clip-on microphone used to record interviews, either connected directly to the camera or via a wireless system. Also called a lapel microphone.

LCD SCREEN: Liquid crystal diodes that light up to produce a color image. The screens are very thin, making them ideal for use on digital cameras. In addition to the viewfinder, many prosumer and professional cameras have "pop-out" LCD screens.

LOCATION: An already existing indoor or outdoor set that has not been created in a studio. Documentaries favor location shooting.

LOWER THIRD: Graphic placed in the lower third portion of the screen, most often to identify a speaker or location.

MEDIUM (PLURAL: MEDIA) Material onto which your movie will be shot or stored such as film, digital video, or capture card.

MICROPHONE: A device for converting sound to electrical impulses that can be recorded and then replayed.

MINIDV: A small-size digital tape format used in consumer and professional digital video cameras.

MONITOR: Television or computer screen. A field monitor is a small, high-resolution, color-corrected screen for checking lighting and exposure on location.

MONOPOD Easily-transported, single-legged camera support used for quick stabilization, usually in conjunction with handheld shooting.

MOS: Motion picture jargon for shooting picture without sound or more specifically without needing to record that sound, so the audio is of no consequence and can be eliminated in editing.

NARRATION: Voice-over, written or otherwise, that describes and tells what is happening. Often used in nature documentaries since critters can't talk.

NATURAL LIGHT: Predominantly refers to sunlight and shooting outside as well as shooting indoors and utilizing windows.

NLE (NON-LINEAR EDITING): Editing system that lets you insert footage anywhere in the edit without having to remove what was there before. Applies to digital and film editing. Think of it as word processing but with video and audio instead of words.

NTSC (NATIONAL TELEVISION STANDARDS COUNCIL): The television and video format used in America and Japan that runs 525 lines at 29.97 or 30 fps.

OPTICAL ZOOM: The range of a lens as defined by the minimum and maximum focal lengths.

PAL (PHASE ALTERNATION LINE): Television and video system used in Europe and other countries that don't use NTSC. Runs 625 lines and 25 fps.

PAN: Following action that moves across the scene, with the camera fixed either on a tripod or handheld.

PIXEL: The smallest unit of a picture that can be controlled. Pixels each have their coordinates and as a whole make up an entire video picture, which consists of thousands of pixels.

POV SHOTS (POINT OF VIEW): Showing on camera/screen what someone is seeing, whether it be a main character or to simply represent the omniscient viewer.

PRESS KIT: Packet of material, whether written or digital, that promotes your documentary/program.

PROPS: Items used by subjects in a film, for example twiddling a pen or writing on a chalkboard.

QUICKTIME: A proprietary multimedia framework developed by Apple that handles various formats of digital video, sound, text, and animation.

REFLECTOR: A shiny surface used to reflect light onto a person or location to boost the existing light and remove shadow areas. Can be used indoors or outdoors.

RGB COLOR MODEL: A process in which red, green, and blue light are added together to reproduce a wide range of colors.

ROUGH CUT: The first edit of the video/film, putting all the elements roughly in the right order.

SCRIPT/SCREENPLAY: The blueprint for a written program, with scene descriptions and narration dialogue.

SHOT LIST: List of shots to be completed for the documentary, usually broken down into a monthly, weekly, and daily schedule. Often made before, during, and after editing!

SOUNDTRACK: Audio part of a video containing all the elements of dialogue, sound effects, and music.

SHORT: A video program that is not feature-length; under 60 minutes.

STATIC SHOT: Scene filmed with the camera in a fixed position, often on a tripod.

STEADICAM: a stabilizing device attached to the camera that is either worn or carried by the camera man to obtain smooth, gliding shots.

STOCK: See *Medium*.

STORYBOARD: Visual representation of the script, using drawings or photos to show key moments of action in a scene. Particularly helpful for re-creations.

SYNC SOUND: When the audio matches up with the video such as when a person is speaking. Usually recorded at the same time.

TALENT RELEASE FORM: A one-page permission slip that your talent/subject signs in which they agree to be videotaped for your specific project. Children under 18 must have it signed by their legal guardian.

TELEPHOTO LENS: Lens with a long focal length that brings everything nearer (like a telescope).

TILT: Following action vertically with the camera mounted on a tripod, such as someone letting go of a helium balloon and then following it up to the sky.

TIME CODE: A sequence of numeric codes used for synchronization of video and audio. Shown as HH:MM:SS:FF (hours:minutes:seconds:frames).

TITLES: Creative way to show the name of the documentary, sometimes including the major credits (producer/director). Can set the tone of the documentary.

TRACK: in editing, this refers to an empty layer in your timeline where you assemble video and audio clips.

TRACKING: A smooth camera movement with the camera mounted on a dolly. See *dolly*.

TRAILER: Short preview of a film showing the best parts to entice the potential viewer.

TRANSITION: How you get from one edited shot to the next, via anything from a cut to a dissolve to an endless number of other possibilities.

TRIPOD: Three-legged camera support with a pan-and-tilt head for smooth shots.

TUNGSTEN: A traditional incandescent light that has its filament made from tungsten, which has a low color temperature that will appear orange with daylight film. The majority of "video lights" are tungsten.

VIDEO: Relating to the visual element of television. Short for videotape. The electronic capturing of images onto videotape.

VOICEOVER: Recorded dialogue that is added to a video/film after it has been shot.

WARDROBE: What your subject/talent is wearing in the shot. Usually representative of them, such as a doctor wearing a white lab coat.

WHITE BALANCE: The control on video cameras that is adjusted to match the light's color temperature and the difference between indoor and outdoor light.

WIDE-ANGLE LENS: A lens with a large field of view. Particular useful for interiors and other confined spaces.

WIDE-SCREEN: A screen ratio where the width is significantly greater than the height. The ratio of 16:9 has been adopted for HD televisions. Some Cinema formats are even wider.

ZEBRA STRIPING: Lines seen through the camera's viewfinder that indicate whether the video is overexposed. It is a useful tool for setting video levels and is not recorded on the video itself.

Index

Resources

KIT AND SOFTWARE

www.adobe.com: Photoshop, Premiere, After Effects

www.apple.com: Macintosh computers. Final Cut, Soundtrack, iMovie, Shake

www.avid.com: Avid editing systems

www.powerproductions.com: Storyboard Quick software

www.frameforge.com: 3D storyboard software

www.canon.com: DV cameras

www.dvfilm.com: Progressive scan after you've shot the movie

www.glidecam.com: Camera stabilizers

www.steadicam.com: Camera stabilizers

www.jvc.com: DV and HDV cameras

www.sony.com: DV, DVCAM, and HDV cameras

www.miller.com.au: fluid-head tripods

www.panasonic.com: DV and HD cameras

USEFUL WEBSITES

www.filmeducation.org: Theory and practice of filmmaking for schools

www.filmmaking.net: Links and resources

www.shootingpeople.org: Networking site for filmmakers

www.withoutabox.com: Film festivals

SUPPORT

www.documentary.org: The website for the International Documentary Association (IDA), a nonprofit membership dedicated to supporting nonfiction filmmakers throughout the world.

www.documentaryfilms.net: A volunteer-driven website devoted to providing documentary film information and resources to both viewers and filmmakers.

www.mediarights.org: A documentary community site that maximizes the impact of social-issue documentaries and shorts to audiences and educators.

www.pbs.org: The official website of the Public Television Service, which has nearly 360 member stations in the United States. It provides a wide array of programming, from news to children's to performance and, most notably, documentaries.

Credits

The author would like to thank the following for their assistance in making this book:

Audra Hartwig, John and Nancy Lindenmuth, Jason Pankoke, Sophie, Michelle Kaffko, Darrell Fusaro, John Borowski, Evan Jacobs, Roy Frumkes, Jessica Gerlach, Nika Offenbac, Jason Kessler, David Gray, Duane Graves, Richard Numeroff, Miles Finlayson, Kartemquin Films, Daniel Marracino, Morgan Spurlock, Brandon Watts, Brett Kelly, Gabe Campisi, and Kate Schwab.

Quarto would like to thank the following agencies for supplying images for inclusion in this book:

p. 2, 5(tl/m), 10, 11, 12, 13, 27, 32, 80, 81, 116, 122, 123 The Kobal Collection; p. 30 Allstar; p. 71(t) Alamy; p. 101 Corbis

All step-by-step and other images are the copyright of Quarto Publishing plc. While every effort has been made to credit contributors, Quarto would like to apologize should there have been any omissions or errors—and would be pleased to make the appropriate correction for future editions of the book.